Editor

Lorin Klistoff, M.A.

Managing Editor

Karen J. Goldfluss, M.S. Ed.

Cover Artist

Brenda DiAntonis

Art Production Manager

Kevin Barnes

Art Coordinator

Renée Christine Yates

Imaging

James Edward Grace

Ricardo Martinez

Publisher

Mary D. Smith, M.S. Ed.

Over 150 nonfiction and fiction passages

Follow-up questions for each passage target essential comprehension skills.

Ideal for test preparation!

Author

Melissa Hart, M.F.A.

Teacher Created Resources, Inc.

12621 Western Avenue

Garden Grove, CA 92841

www.teachercreated.com

ISBN: 978-1-4206-3487-7

©2006 Teacher Created Resources, Inc.

Reprinted, 2020

Made in U.S.A.

The classroom teacher may reproduce the materials in this book for use in a single classroom only. The reproduction of any part of this book for other classrooms or for an entire school or school system is strictly prohibited. No part of this publication may be transmitted or recorded in any form without written permission from the publisher.

Table of Contents

Great-horned Owls—Cats—The Crow—The Polar Bear—Dogs—Emperor Penguin—Gila Monster—Millipedes—Ivory-Billed Woodpecker—Peregrine Falcon—Anteater—Stinkbug—Giant Panda—Black Widow—Giraffe

The Ocean—Mountains—Trees—Rivers—Deserts—Wetlands—Glaciers—Rainforests—Volcanoes—Canyons—Earthquakes—Tornadoes—Hurricanes—Tsunami—Blizzards

Sun, Earth, and Moon—Fossils—Worms—Trees—Lightning—Butterfly—Fall Leaves—Where Animals Go—Stars—The Moon—Sharks—The Food Chain—Venus Fly Trap—Dust—Rainbows—Inventions

American Colonies—Betsy Ross—The Bald Eagle—Bison—Uncle Sam—Yankee Doodle—Johnny Appleseed—Fireworks—George Washington—Abe Lincoln—Sacagawea—Harriet Tubman—The Mayans—Space Travel

Germs—Exercise—Healthy Food—Ears—Lungs—Sleep—Water—Teeth—Bones—Common Cold—Chicken Pox—Eyes—Getting Mad—Bruises—Laughter—Allergies—Foods with Color—Talk It Out

Table of Contents

Reading provides a wealth of new ideas for students. This book will improve reading and comprehension skills through ongoing practice. Regular exposure to comprehending the written word allows students to become better at both reading and critical thinking. *Daily Warm-Ups: Reading* (*Grade 1*) contains passages to be read on a daily basis, followed by related questions based on Bloom's Taxonomy which allows for practice in high-level comprehension. Teachers who incorporate this book into part of their daily classroom agenda will find dramatic improvement in students' abilities to read and comprehend passages of writing.

Nonfiction and Fiction

Daily Warm-Ups: Reading is divided into two sections—nonfiction and fiction. Students benefit from being exposed to a variety of reading genres. The nonfiction section of this book is divided into five categories relating to animals, geography, science, American history, and health and wellness. Students will explore a variety of nonfiction topics and learn to consider each critically through questions following each passage.

The fiction section of the book includes fairy tales and folklore, historical fiction, contemporary realistic fiction, mystery/suspense/adventure, and fantasy. Questions follow each story to stimulate further analysis of plot, characters, setting, and theme.

Comprehension Questions

Solid comprehension is the goal of any reading assignment. The student who can read and comprehend a passage skillfully performs well on tests and critical thinking assignments. As importantly, these students take pleasure in reading. The questions following each passage encourage students to look beyond the words on a page and investigate topics and themes deeply. In addition, passages are designed to offer new vocabulary, which students may incorporate into their own writing and discussion. Questions in *Daily Warm-Ups: Reading* will help students to do the following:

* Recognize the main idea

* Identify details

* Recall details

* Summarize passages

* Describe characters and character traits

* Classify and sort into categories

* Compare and contrast

* Make generalizations

* Draw conclusions

* Recognize facts and fiction

* Apply information to new situation

* Recognize a sequence of events

* Understand new vocabulary

Readability

Each of the reading passages in *Daily Warm-Ups: Reading (Grade 1)* varies in difficulty to meet the various reading levels of your students. The passages have been categorized as follows: below grade level, at grade level, and above grade level. (See Leveling Chart on page 175.)

Record Keeping

Use the tracking sheet on page 6 to record which warm-up exercises you have given to your students. Or, distribute copies of the sheet for students to keep their own records. Use the certificate on page 176 as you see fit. You can use the certificate as a reward for students completing a certain number of warm-up exercises. Or, you may choose to distribute the certificates to students who complete the warm-up exercises with 100% accuracy.

How to Make the Most of This Book

Here are ideas to consider as you begin *Daily Warm-Ups: Reading* with your students:

- Read through the book so that you are familiar with each section. Explain to students that the book is divided into nonfiction and fiction, with various subgenres.

- Model the way in which you want your students to work through the entire process of reading the passage and answering the questions. Narrate your own process out loud once, so that students may establish their own successful practice of reading and critical thinking.

- Clarify that students are to answer questions following each passage with complete sentences and correct spelling and punctuation.

- Upon completing the first reading assignment, students should turn in their work for an initial assessment. Praise successful work and address any errors immediately.

- Set aside a particular time during each day to complete a reading passage and answer the comprehension questions. Once you have established a regular routine, students will grow to expect and enjoy their daily reading task.

- Encourage your students during each reading period, and provide positive reinforcement so that they will view reading as a pleasurable activity.

- Be aware that students read at varying levels. Some students may need extra time and attention with the material. You may want to assign small groups of students to complete comprehension questions together one time. This allows for greater independence and confidence during the next reading assignment. Likewise, be aware of students who may read at a higher level. You may want to assign an extra-credit paragraph of further analysis for students who need an additional challenge.

Tracking Sheet

NONFICTION

Animals		Geography		Science		Amercian History		Health and Wellness	
Page 9		Page 24		Page 39		Page 55		Page 69	
Page 10		Page 25		Page 40		Page 56		Page 70	
Page 11		Page 26		Page 41		Page 57		Page 71	
Page 12		Page 27		Page 42		Page 58		Page 72	
Page 13		Page 28		Page 43		Page 59		Page 73	
Page 14		Page 29		Page 44		Page 60		Page 74	
Page 15		Page 30		Page 45		Page 61		Page 75	
Page 16		Page 31		Page 46		Page 62		Page 76	
Page 17		Page 32		Page 47		Page 63		Page 77	
Page 18		Page 33		Page 48		Page 64		Page 78	
Page 19		Page 34		Page 49		Page 65		Page 79	
Page 20		Page 35		Page 50		Page 66		Page 80	
Page 21		Page 36		Page 51		Page 67		Page 81	
Page 22		Page 37		Page 52		Page 68		Page 82	
Page 23		Page 38		Page 53				Page 83	
				Page 54				Page 84	
								Page 85	
								Page 86	

FICTION

Fairy Tales and Folklore		Historical Fiction		Contemporary Realistic Fiction		Mystery/Suspense/ Adventure		Fantasy	
Page 89		Page 104		Page 120		Page 135		Page 151	
Page 90		Page 105		Page 121		Page 136		Page 152	
Page 91		Page 106		Page 122		Page 137		Page 153	
Page 92		Page 107		Page 123		Page 138		Page 154	
Page 93		Page 108		Page 124		Page 139		Page 155	
Page 94		Page 109		Page 125		Page 140		Page 156	
Page 95		Page 110		Page 126		Page 141		Page 157	
Page 96		Page 111		Page 127		Page 142		Page 158	
Page 97		Page 112		Page 128		Page 143		Page 159	
Page 98		Page 113		Page 129		Page 144		Page 160	
Page 99		Page 114		Page 130		Page 145		Page 161	
Page 100		Page 115		Page 131		Page 146		Page 162	
Page 101		Page 116		Page 132		Page 147		Page 163	
Page 102		Page 117		Page 133		Page 148		Page 164	
Page 103		Page 118		Page 134		Page 149		Page 165	
		Page 119				Page 150		Page 166	

NONFICTION

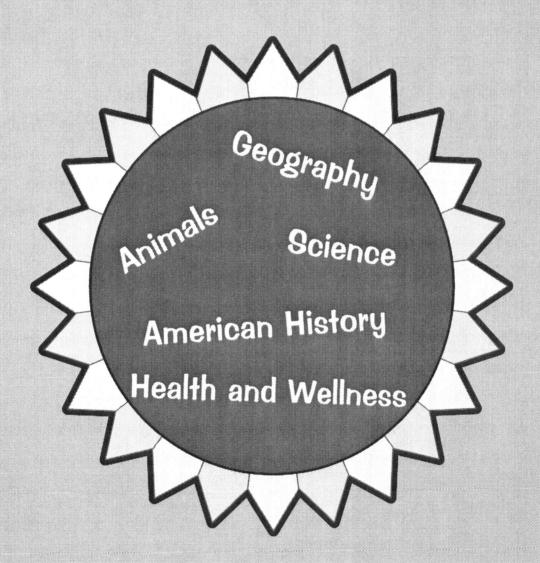

Geography

Animals   Science

American History

Health and Wellness

8

©Teacher Created Resources, Inc.

DAILY
Warm-Up 1

Name _____ Date _____

GREAT-HORNED OWLS

Have you ever heard a hoot as the sun goes down? This may be the cry of a great-horned owl. She is looking for her dinner.

Great-horned owls have sharp eyes and ears. They see and hear small animals. Then, they <u>swoop</u> down and grab their prey.

Great-horned owls eat mice, frogs, snakes, and small birds. They also eat insects. They can fly without making a sound.

Great-horned owls hoot to other owls in the forest. Their brown and black feathers make them hard to see in the daytime. You may see one flying at dawn or dusk. Be very quiet. Then, you may hear owls calling out to each other through the trees.

STORY QUESTIONS

1. In this passage, the word *swoop* means . . .

    a. run.   c. skip.

    b. fly.   d. skate.

2. Which statement is **false**?

    a. Great-horned owls don't see well.

    b. Great-horned owls fly in silence.

    c. Great-horned owls eat snakes.

    d. Great-horned owls have feathers.

3. What colors are the great-horned owl's feathers?

    a. black and white   c. brown and orange

    b. blue and red   d. brown and black

4. Which animal does the great-horned owl **not** eat?

    a. frog   c. small bird

    b. snake   d. bear

DAILY Warm-Up 2

Name _____

Date _____

CATS

Do you have a cat at home? If so, you know what amazing creatures they are.

Cats learn about the weather from their whiskers. They can tell if it is hot or cold, wet or dry. Their whiskers also help them to find their way in the dark.

Indoor cats like to play with balls. They also love to play with string. You can toss a catnip mouse and train your cat to bring it back to you.

One of the best things about cats is their fur. They keep themselves very clean. They are soft and warm. Most cats like to be brushed and petted. They also like to sit on your lap.

Many cats do not have a home. They are cold and hungry. You can adopt one from your local shelter. Then, you will have an amazing creature of your own.

STORY QUESTIONS

1. Cats learn about the weather from their . . .
   a. tails.
   b. fur.
   c. whiskers.
   d. teeth.

2. You can train your cat to . . .
   a. cook dinner.
   b. bring back a catnip mouse.
   c. brush your hair.
   d. play football.

3. How do you think a cat cleans its fur?
   a. by taking a shower
   b. by swimming in the ocean
   c. by soaking in the bathtub
   d. by licking itself

4. In this story, the word *shelter* means . . .
   a. a place that holds stray cats.
   b. a teepee.
   c. a doghouse.
   d. a tent.

DAILY Name _____ **Date** _____

Warm-Up 3

THE CROW

You can find crows almost any place. These birds are very smart. They can even talk!

Crows can live in forests. They can live near houses. They can even live in big cities. They eat bugs, berries, fruit, and scraps of food.

Crows have large brains. They hide bits of food and save them for later. They can learn how to crack nuts. They even make tools out of twigs.

Crows talk to each other. They caw and squeak. They can learn human language, too. Some crows can learn to ring a bell when asked. Others can laugh <u>on command</u>. Crows are interesting birds!

STORY QUESTIONS

1. Why do you think crows can live almost any place?
   a. They carry big suitcases.
   b. They can eat many different types of food.
   c. They like to ride the subway.
   d. They steal people's beds.

2. Which statement is **true**?
   a. Crows can learn to drive a car.   c. Crows can make their own tools.
   b. Crows can live on the moon.   d. Crows are not very smart.

3. In this story, the words *on command* mean . . .
   a. when asked to do so.   c. when thrown in jail.
   b. when forced to do so.   d. when someone says "pretty please."

4. Why would a crow need to make a tool?
   a. to fix its car   c. to record itself laughing
   b. to repair a sink   d. to get bugs out of the cracks in trees

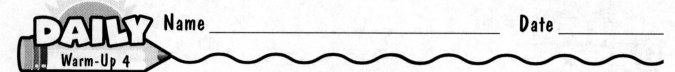

Name _____   Date _____

THE POLAR BEAR

The polar bear makes its home in the cold and icy Arctic. Other animals might freeze or starve. But the polar bear knows how to live in the snow.

Polar bears have thick blubber, or fat, that protects them from the cold. They also have a thick fur coat.

The polar bear's coat is white. This allows it to blend into the snow. That way, the polar bear can sneak up on its prey.

Polar bears swim well. They eat seals, walruses, small whales, and rodents. In the summer, they may eat berries.

Polar bears will also eat people. They may look cute and furry, but be careful of this big bear!

STORY QUESTIONS

1. Polar bears are found in . . .
   a. sunny Florida.
   b. tropical jungles.
   c. the freezing Arctic.
   d. the Pacific Ocean.

2. Polar bears can live in the cold because . . .
   a. they have fireplaces.
   b. they have thick fur coats.
   c. they wear socks.
   d. they eat blubber for lunch.

3. Which sentence is **true**?
   a. Polar bears blend into the snow.
   b. Polar bears are black.
   c. Polar bears blend into brown rocks.
   d. Polar bears are white and black.

4. Which of the following do polar bears not eat?
   a. people
   b. walruses
   c. rodents
   d. salad

Name _____   **Date** _____

DOGS

Have you ever shaken hands with a dog? If so, you know that most dogs love people. They will do tricks and even help in a <u>crisis</u>.

Dogs are very nice. They make loyal friends. Many dogs are happy as pets. They love to be with people and do tricks.

You can teach a dog to shake hands. Dogs can jump through hoops. They can roll over. They can also fetch a stick. They are very smart animals.

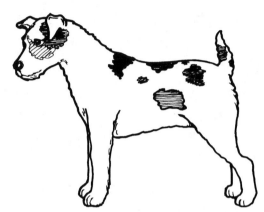

Dogs can also rescue people. Some dogs bark if a stranger enters the house. Other dogs save people from fires. Police dogs help to <u>fight crime</u>.

Dogs are wonderful animals. Adopt one, and you will have a friend for life!

STORY QUESTIONS

1. In this story, the word *crisis* means . . .

   a. spilled milk.
   c. a stubbed toe.
   b. an emergency.
   d. running out of gas.

2. Which statement is **true**?

   a. Dogs are mean.
   c. Dogs are our enemies.
   b. Dogs do not like people.
   d. Dogs make good friends.

3. What trick is a dog unable to do?

   a. shake hands
   c. drive a truck
   b. fetch a stick
   d. jump through a hoop

4. What does the phrase "fight crime" mean?

   a. to punch a robber in the face
   b. to beat up a criminal
   c. to kick and scratch a bully
   d. to keep people safe from danger

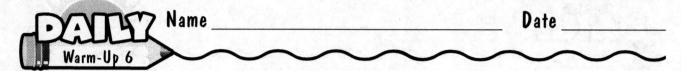

Name _____   Date _____

EMPEROR PENGUIN

Emperor Penguins can't fly, but they can dive and swim. They can also walk miles and miles over ice and snow.

The Emperor Penguin lives in Antarctica. These penguins can dive far down into the ocean.

Emperor Penguins can hold their breath for 20 minutes. They can swim very fast after their <u>prey</u>. They eat fish and squid.

Every spring Emperor Penguins walk far across snow and ice. Then, they lay their eggs. Males care for the eggs. Females leave to find food. Later, they come back to feed the new babies.

Even though they can't fly, Emperor Penguins are amazing birds.

STORY QUESTIONS

1. What does the word *prey* mean in this story?
   a. to sit with your hands together   c. food
   b. to ask for something   d. eggs

2. What would be another good name for this story?
   a. "Too Bad They Can't Fly"   c. "Warm-Weather Birds"
   b. "The Amazing Emperor Penguin"   d. "Fish are Great"

3. Who cares for the Emperor Penguin's eggs?
   a. the squid   c. no one
   b. the female penguin   d. the male penguin

4. Which statement is a fact?
   a. Female penguins feed their new babies.
   b. Male penguins abandon their babies.
   c. Female penguins don't like their babies.
   d. Mother and father penguins can fly.

Name _____   **Date** _____

DAILY Warm-Up 7

GILA MONSTER

The Gila monster is a large lizard. You can say its name like this—"Heela." It is pretty. But it is also scary.

The Gila monster lives in the desert. Its skin is black, pink, orange, and yellow.

The Gila monster is two feet long. It walks slowly. It eats rodents, small birds, and eggs.

This lizard has poison in its teeth. It won't kill you. Still, the Gila monster bites people. It can hold on tight to a leg or arm with its teeth. Be careful!

STORY QUESTIONS

1. How do you pronounce *Gila*?
   a. Gee-la   c. Guy-la
   b. Heela   d. Hilla

2. Why is the Gila monster scary?
   a. because it lives in the desert   c. because it walks slowly
   b. because it eats eggs   d. because it has a poisonous bite

3. The Gila monster holds poison in its . . .
   a. teeth.   c. eyes.
   b. tail.   d. claws.

4. Why should you be careful around Gila monsters?
   a. because they move quickly
   b. because they eat rodents
   c. because they bite and hold on tight to people
   d. because they are black, pink, orange, and yellow

Name _____

Date _____

MILLIPEDES

The millipede is small but strong. It can have between 80 and 400 legs!

Millipedes walk slowly. Still, they can dig long tunnels. They wave their legs and push underground head first.

These creatures eat dead leaves and plants. They wet the food and <u>scrape</u> at it with their jaws.

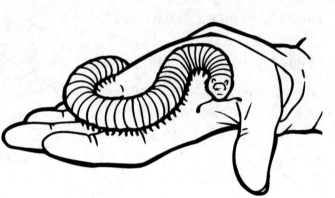

When scared, the millipede curls into a ball. Its back is hard, like armor. This protects its legs. Millipedes also have poison. It burns ants, but it doesn't hurt people.

Never step on a millipede. It has places to go and tunnels to dig!

STORY QUESTIONS

1. How many legs can a millipede have?
   a. 40
   b. 90
   c. 600
   d. 10

2. How do millipedes dig tunnels?
   a. with a shovel
   b. with their teeth
   c. with their legs and heads
   d. with a spoon

3. In this story, *scrape* means . . .
   a. to gnaw at something.
   b. to skin your knee.
   c. to carve a branch.
   d. to get into trouble.

4. Why should you never step on a millipede?
   a. because it burns ants
   b. because it has lots of legs
   c. because it has tunnels to dig
   d. because it curls into a ball

Name _____   **Date** _____

IVORY-BILLED WOODPECKER

For many years, people thought the ivory-billed woodpecker was gone. In 2005, a man saw one.

Ivory-billed woodpeckers are almost two feet long. They have a white bill. Males also have red feathers on the top of their heads. They have large, curved claws.

The ivory-billed woodpecker uses its <u>bill</u> to find food. It peels the bark off trees to uncover bugs. Its bill makes a knocking sound against the wood.

Long ago, people hunted these birds. They also cut down trees. These trees were home to the ivory-billed woodpecker. Soon, these birds disappeared.

Recently, scientists have found at least one male bird in an Arkansas swamp. Welcome back, ivory-billed woodpecker!

STORY QUESTIONS

1. What is **true** about ivory-billed woodpeckers?

    a. They are tiny birds.   c. They eat watermelon.

    b. They are all gone.   d. One was discovered in a swamp.

2. In this story, the word *bill* means . . .

    a. a dollar.   c. a beak.

    b. a law.   d. a notice sent in the mail.

3. How do ivory-billed woodpeckers use their bills?

    a. They use it to uncover bugs.

    b. They use it to dig holes in the sand.

    c. They use it to pop balloons.

    d. They use it to talk to bugs.

4. Why did these birds disappear?

    a. They moved to Italy.   c. They lost their homes.

    b. They all got sick.   d. They got lost in swamps.

DAILY Warm-Up 10

Name _____ Date _____

PEREGRINE FALCON

The peregrine falcon is the fastest animal on the earth. These lovely birds are fierce hunters.

The peregrine falcon has blue-gray wings. They have white faces with a black stripe on each cheek. Their wingspan is about three feet.

This falcon eats other birds. It likes pigeons, starlings, parrots, and ducks. It flies high in the sky. When it sees a bird, it goes into a dive. This is called a <u>stoop</u>.

Peregrine falcons can dive at over 200 miles per hour! They ball up their feet. Then, they knock prey out in midair.

Most young peregrine falcons die in their first year. Animals steal baby chicks and eggs. Pesticides also hurt these falcons.

People are helping to save peregrine falcons. Now, there are many pairs of these birds. Some of them live in cities. They make nests on high bridges and skyscrapers. Have you seen one?

STORY QUESTIONS

1. The peregrine falcon is famous for its . . .
   a. stripes.   c. smile.
   b. speed.   d. nest.

2. In this story, the word *stoop* means . . .
   a. something to sit on.   c. dive.
   b. duck.   d. bend down to pick up something.

3. Why do peregrine falcons die in their first year?
   a. Animals steal baby chicks from their parents.
   b. They fly into rocks.
   c. Parrots eat them.
   d. They live on bridges.

4. You may spot the nest of a peregrine falcon on a . . .
   a. bus.   c. apple tree.
   b. boat.   d. high bridge.

DAILY Name _____ Date _____

Warm-Up 11

ANTEATER

What animal likes to eat ants? An anteater, of course!

Anteaters like swamps and forests. They live in South America. They like hot weather.

Anteaters have sharp claws. They can climb trees. Their claws are also weapons in case of an attack.

They also have long, sticky tongues. Anteaters use their tongues to pick up food. First, they open an ant nest. Then, they scoop up ants with their tongue.

Big anteaters are four feet long. Small anteaters are the size of a rat. Big or small, they all love to eat ants.

STORY QUESTIONS

1. How do you think anteaters got their name?
   a. They love to eat ants.   c. Ants love to eat them.
   b. They like to play with ants.   d. Ants like to climb trees.

2. What is a fact about anteaters?
   a. They don't have claws.   c. They live in North America.
   b. They like hot weather.   d. They scoop up ants with their tails.

3. Anteaters climb trees using their . . .
   a. tails.   c. ants.
   b. tongues.   d. claws.

4. The smallest anteater is the size of a . . .
   a. rat.
   b. man.
   c. whale.
   d. cow.

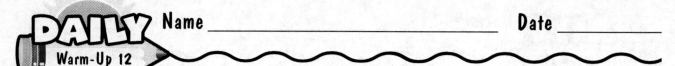

Name _____ **Date** _____

STINKBUG

One bug leaves a bad <u>smell</u> wherever it goes. It is the stinkbug.

Stinkbugs are broad, flat insects. They can be green, gray, and brown. They can even be red.

Stinkbugs smell. This bad odor protects them from enemies. When they walk across a leaf, the leaf smells bad, too.

There are 5,000 kinds of stinkbugs. Some stinkbugs eat plant juice. Others eat insects. No matter what they eat, they stink!

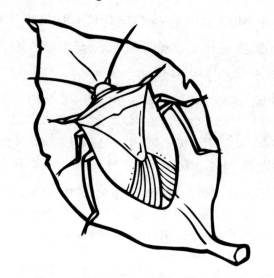

STORY QUESTIONS

1. Stinkbugs can be . . .
   a. sweet-smelling.   c. green.
   b. purple.   d. delicious.

2. In this story, *smell* means
   a. sniff.   c. inhale.
   b. snort.   d. stink.

3. The stinkbug's smell protects it from . . .
   a. plants.   c. leaves.
   b. enemies.   d. juice.

4. Which sentence is a fact?
   a. There are 5,000 kinds of stinkbugs.
   b. There are two kinds of stinkbugs.
   c. Some stinkbugs eat elephants.
   d. Stinkbugs smell good.

DAILY **Name** _____ **Date** _____

Warm-Up 13

GIANT PANDA

The Giant Panda is a beautiful bear. It is also rare.

Giant Pandas are black and white. They have black spots over their eyes. They have a short tail. They have paws with five fingers.

Giant Pandas eat bamboo plants. Sometimes they eat bugs, eggs, and fish.

Very few Giant Pandas live in the wild. People build near their homes. They don't have many babies.

All over, groups try to <u>save</u> this beautiful bear.

STORY QUESTIONS

1. Which of the sentences below is **true**?
   a. Giant Pandas have hands.
   b. Giant Pandas have white spots over their eyes.
   c. Giant Pandas are rare.
   d. There are many Giant Pandas in the wild.

2. What do Giant Pandas eat?
   a. tacos   c. pizza
   b. bamboo   d. egg salad

3. Why aren't there many Giant Pandas?
   a. They don't have many babies.   c. They eat bamboo.
   b. They fight all the time.   d. They have five fingers.

4. In this story, *save* means . . .
   a. bank.   c. store.
   b. keep.   d. protect.

DAILY Name _____ Date _____
Warm-Up 14

BLACK WIDOW

What spider has a red spot that means poison? The black widow.

The female black widow is black and shiny. She has a red spot. The male black widow is smaller. He is dark brown with a yellow spot.

Black widows are poisonous. They catch insects in their webs. Then, they sting them and eat them.

The bite of a black widow can hurt people. Some get very sick. A few die.

Black widows have many babies. Females live a long time. Males do not. Sometimes the females eat the males.

If you see a red spot on a black spider, be careful!

STORY QUESTIONS

1. Which statement is **true**?
   a. The male black widow lives longer than the female.
   b. The female black widow has a red spot.
   c. The male black widow has a red spot.
   d. The female black widow doesn't live long.

2. How do black widows catch food?
   a. They go fishing.   c. They use a catcher's mitt.
   b. They hold out their hands.   d. They build webs.

3. What could happen if a black widow bites you?
   a. You could get sick.   c. You could eat insects.
   b. You could turn black.   d. You could make a web.

4. What should you do if you see a black widow?
   a. walk away   c. eat it
   b. pick it up   d. touch it with your finger

DAILY Name _____ Date _____
Warm-Up 15

GIRAFFE

The giraffe is famous for its long neck. We also know it because of its spots.

Wild giraffes live in Africa. They are very tall. They eat leaves high up in trees.

The giraffe has a long, sticky tongue. It uses its tongue to clean bugs off its face. It also has a big heart. A giraffe's heart can weigh 24 pounds!

Giraffes can run fast. They kick with strong legs. They need only an hour of sleep each day.

You can see giraffes in the zoo. You can also see them on a trip to Africa.

STORY QUESTIONS

1. The giraffe is famous for . . .
   a. its long nose.
   b. its short neck.
   c. its long tail.
   d. its long neck.

2. The giraffe uses its tongue to . . .
   a. eat ants off leaves.
   b. clean bugs off its face.
   c. clean its tail.
   d. run fast.

3. How can a giraffe hurt its enemy?
   a. It can lick enemies in the face.
   b. It can run away.
   c. It can climb trees.
   d. It can kick enemies with strong legs.

4. Where can you see giraffes?
   a. in a zoo
   b. in Texas
   c. in the mall
   d. in bed

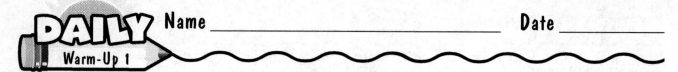

Name _____ **Date** _____

THE OCEAN

The ocean is made up of salt water. There are four main oceans. They are the Pacific, the Atlantic, the Indian, and the Arctic Ocean.

The top of the earth is made up mostly of ocean. Many fish and plants live in the ocean. Sharks swim through the water. Whales and seals live in the ocean, too.

The ocean gives us fish for food. It lets us sail boats from one place to another place. We can even surf on ocean waves.

We need the ocean in order to live. You can help to keep the beach clean when you visit. Then, we can all enjoy the ocean.

STORY QUESTIONS

1. What is the ocean made up of?
   a. sharks   c. boats
   b. salt water   d. plants

2. What does not live in the ocean?
   a. sharks   c. tigers
   b. whales   d. fish

3. Why do we need the ocean?
   a. It gives us food.   c. It is cold.
   b. It is pretty.   d. It is big.

4. How can you help the ocean?
   a. You can surf.
   b. You can sail.
   c. You can fish.
   d. You can keep the beach clean.

DAILY Name _____ Date _____
Warm-Up 2

MOUNTAINS

A mountain is a very tall hill. It climbs high into the sky. There are mountains all over the world.

The tallest mountain in the world is Mount Everest. It is in Nepal. People climb to its top. It is very cold.

The highest mountain in the U.S. is in Alaska. People call it Denali. It is lovely.

Mountains are fun to explore. Bears and birds live there. So do trees and plants. Have you ever walked up a mountain?

STORY QUESTIONS

1. A mountain is a very tall . . .
   a. bear.   c. hill.
   b. tree.   d. plant.

2. If you walk up Mount Everest, you need a . . .
   a. swim suit.   c. pair of sandals.
   b. bear.   d. snow suit.

3. The highest mountain in the U.S. is in . . .
   a. Nepal.   c. New York.
   b. Alaska.   d. California.

4. What does not live on a mountain?
   a. whales
   b. birds
   c. trees
   d. bears

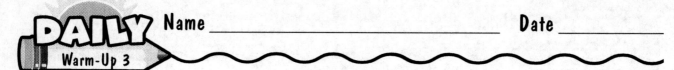

Name _____ **Date** _____

DAILY Warm-Up 3

TREES

A tree is a tall, woody plant. Some trees can grow to 350 feet. Trees can live for thousands of years.

Trees have a few parts. They have a <u>trunk</u>. They have branches. They also have roots.

Some trees have needles. These trees are called evergreens. Some of these are pine, fir, spruce, and cedar.

Other trees have leaves. Some of these are elm, maple, ash, and apple. These leaves turn red and yellow in the fall.

We need trees. They give us air. They also give us shade. Some trees give us fruit. So plant a tree today!

STORY QUESTIONS

1. In this story, the word *trunk* means . . .
   a. suitcase.
   b. the nose on an elephant.
   c. a woody stem.
   d. a chest.

2. Trees with needles are called . . .
   a. evergreens.
   b. trunks.
   c. wood.
   d. elm.

3. What color are maple leaves in the fall?
   a. blue
   b. red
   c. purple
   d. black

4. Trees do not give us . . .
   a. fruit.
   b. shade.
   c. air.
   d. dogs.

   ©Teacher Created Resources, Inc.

DAILY Name _____   **Date** _____

Warm-Up 4

RIVERS

We need rivers. They bring water from mountains to oceans. They also bring water to lakes.

Snow falls on mountains. Then it melts. The water runs down the mountain. Now, it becomes a river. It travels to oceans or lakes.

The longest river in the world is the Nile. It is in Africa. You can take a boat down the Nile.

Some rivers flood. This can be good for farmland. But it is bad if a river floods your house. Some people pollute rivers. This hurts the water, plants, and animals.

Do you have a river in your town? Where did it come from? You can help to keep it clean. Pick up trash in the river. Thank it for bringing you water.

STORY QUESTIONS

1. Rivers bring water to . . .
   a. lakes.
   b. mountains.
   c. floods.
   d. trash.

2. What happens to snow when it melts?
   a. It floods.
   b. It pollutes water.
   c. It runs down mountains.
   d. It hurts animals.

3. Where is the longest river?
   a. in the mountains
   b. in California
   c. in the ocean
   d. in Africa

4. How can you help to keep a river clean?
   a. pick up animals
   b. pick up trash
   c. pick up water
   d. pick up boats

DAILY Warm-Up 5

Name _____

Date _____

DESERTS

Can you live in the desert? Yes, but it can be very hot. It can also be very cold.

Deserts are made up of sand or rock. Some do not get much rain. Others are covered in frozen snow. These deserts are called tundra.

Plants can live in the desert. They <u>store</u> water in their roots and leaves. The cactus is a desert plant. It can live for 200 years. Birds live in holes in the cactus.

People can live in the desert, too. But, watch out for the hot sun and always carry water!

STORY QUESTIONS

1. Deserts can be very . . .
   a. rainy.
   b. hot.
   c. ugly.
   d. wet.

2. Tundra is a desert that is covered in . . .
   a. rocks.
   b. sand.
   c. leaves.
   d. snow.

3. What lives in the cactus?
   a. birds
   b. snow
   c. water
   d. tundra

4. In this story, *store* means . . .
   a. a place to shop.
   b. a market.
   c. groceries.
   d. save.

DAILY Warm-Up 6   Name _____   Date _____

WETLANDS

How are a bog, a marsh, and a swamp the same? They are all wetlands.

A wetland is land that is very wet at least some of the time. Plants and animals live there.

The crocodile lives in swamps in Florida. A yellow fly lives in bogs in England. This fly is called the "hairy canary."

People are working to save the wetlands. They try not to build houses on them. They also try not to build roads over them.

Wild grass and birds and bugs live in wetlands. We must keep their homes safe.

STORY QUESTIONS

1. What is not a kind of wetland?
   a. a bog
   b. a marsh
   c. an ocean
   d. a swamp

2. A wetland is land that is wet . . .
   a. all the time.
   b. some of the time.
   c. never.
   d. in the spring.

3. The hairy canary is a . . .
   a. crocodile.
   b. wetland.
   c. wild grass.
   d. fly.

4. We should protect wetlands to . . .
   a. keep plants and animals safe.
   b. build roads over.
   c. build houses on.
   d. drink water.

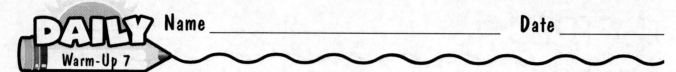

GLACIERS

What do you call a long, blue river of ice? A glacier!

Most fresh water on Earth is in glaciers. Some glaciers never melt. You can find glaciers in the mountains. Others <u>cover</u> big areas of continents. They are home to snow fleas and ice worms.

The top part of a glacier is snow. The middle part is mixed snow and ice. The bottom part is ice.

You can take a class to learn how to walk on a glacier. You need special boots. You also need a rope and an ice axe. Then, you can walk on a river of ice!

STORY QUESTIONS

1. Where is most fresh water on Earth?

a. in oceans

b. in lakes

c. in rivers

d. in glaciers

2. In this story, the word *cover* means . . .

a. spread over.

b. a bedspread.

c. a quilt.

d. put your hands over your head.

3. Glaciers are made up of . . .

a. snow, ice, and sand.

b. snow and ice.

c. snow, fleas, and ice worms.

d. rivers and mountains.

4. What do you need to walk on a glacier?

a. slippers and a rope

b. boots and an ice axe

c. snow fleas

d. boots and a raft

DAILY Name _____ **Date** _____
Warm-Up 8

RAINFORESTS

Rainforests give us air. They give us plants and animals and medicine.

A rainforest has many trees. It gets a lot of rain. Many kinds of animals and plants live here.

Wild pigs live in rainforests. So do snakes. It is also home to bugs and birds.

Trees here can grow to be 150 feet tall. Plants have big, bright flowers. Some rainforests are home to tall bamboo.

People make pills out of tree <u>bark</u> and plants in the rainforest. These pills help many people. We must save our rainforests.

STORY QUESTIONS

1. Rainforests do not give us . . .
   a. plants.
   b. medicine.
   c. bamboo.
   d. burgers.

2. What animals live in rainforests?
   a. whales
   b. wild pigs
   c. sharks
   d. ice worms

3. In this story, the word *bark* means . . .
   a. what a dog says.
   b. to skin your knee.
   c. a tree covering.
   d. woof.

4. The rainforest gives people . . .
   a. medicine.
   b. snow.
   c. ice.
   d. sand.

Name _____   Date _____

VOLCANOES

Where does the word *volcano* come from? It comes from the Roman god of fire. His name was Vulcan.

A volcano is a mountain that blows its top! Hot lava pushes through the mountain. Then, it flows down the side.

Some volcanoes are millions of years old. Some sleep. Others are active. It is <u>hard</u> to tell when a volcano will blow.

Many volcanoes have snow. If they blow their tops, hot lava melts the snow. It burns up trees and plants, too, just like a fire.

STORY QUESTIONS

1. The word *volcano* comes from the Roman god of . . .
   a. heat.   c. fire.
   b. burn.   d. sun.

2. What pushes through a mountain to make a volcano?
   a. ice   c. snow
   b. fire   d. lava

3. In this story, the word *hard* means . . .
   a. difficult.   c. wood.
   b. solid.   d. mean.

4. Who is Vulcan?
   a. a volcano
   b. a tree
   c. a mountain
   d. a Roman god

32   ©Teacher Created Resources, Inc.

DAILY Warm-Up 10

Name _____ Date _____

CANYONS

Have you ever heard of the <u>Grand</u> Canyon? It is one of the largest canyons in the world.

A canyon is a deep crack in the earth. There are cliffs on each side. Sometimes, a river flows through it.

Many animals live in canyons. Grey squirrels make their homes there. Rabbits and mice live there. So do hawks and owls. Long ago, people used to live in caves above canyons.

The Grand Canyon is pretty. It is red and orange and yellow. You can take a train to see it. You can ride a mule down to the bottom of it. You can even raft on the river that goes through the Grand Canyon.

STORY QUESTIONS

1. In this story, the word *grand* means . . .

   a. small.　　　　　　　　c. large.

   b. tiny.　　　　　　　　　d. ugly.

2. On each side of a canyon, you will see . . .

   a. cliffs.　　　　　　　　c. mountains.

   b. rivers.　　　　　　　　d. trains.

3. Who used to live in caves?

   a. mules　　　　　　　　c. owls

   b. rafts　　　　　　　　　d. people

4. What can you ride to the bottom of the Grand Canyon?

   a. a train

   b. a mule

   c. a river

   d. a rabbit

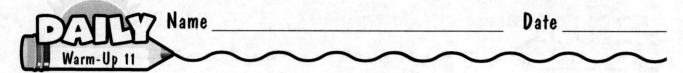

Name _____ Date _____

EARTHQUAKES

The floor shakes. Dishes fall and break. It's an earthquake!

The surface of the earth has plates. These <u>plates</u> bump into each other. Then, there is an earthquake.

Earthquakes can be small. Others are big. They knock down houses. They also knock down trees.

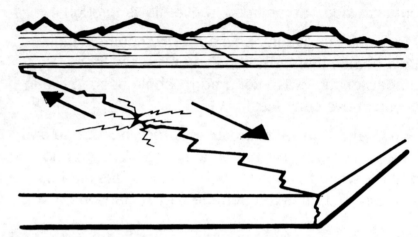

Earthquakes mean danger. When you feel one, get under a table or desk. Cover your head with your hands. Stay calm. Soon, the shaking will stop.

STORY QUESTIONS

1. In this story, *plates* mean . . .
- a. dishes.
- b. rocks in the earth.
- c. bowls.
- d. floor.

2. Earthquakes happen when . . .
- a. dishes break.
- b. houses fall.
- c. floors shake.
- d. plates in the earth bump into each other.

3. If there is an earthquake, get under a . . .
- a. table.
- b. tree.
- c. house.
- d. floor.

4. In an earthquake, you should . . .
- a. go outside.
- b. cry.
- c. stay calm.
- d. bump into each other.

DAILY Name _____ **Date** _____
Warm-Up 12

TORNADOES

Have you ever seen a cloud that spins? This is a tornado.

Tornadoes come from storms. Wind blows a cloud across the land. It can blow 300 miles per hour.

Tornadoes can hit the earth. They pick up houses and cars. Then, they drop them somewhere else.

Most tornadoes happen during spring and summer. If a tornado comes to town, go to the safest place you can with an adult.

Come out when the tornado is gone. Tornadoes can damage houses and hurt animals and people. Be careful!

STORY QUESTIONS

1. A tornado is a cloud that . . .
   a. dances.
   b. runs.
   c. spins.
   d. hits.

2. Tornadoes can blow . . .
   a. 300 miles an hour.
   b. 30 miles an hour.
   c. 3,000 miles an hour.
   d. 3 miles an hour.

3. Most tornadoes are in . . .
   a. winter.
   b. spring.
   c. fall and summer.
   d. spring and summer.

4. In a tornado, you should stay in . . .
   a. a tree.
   b. a safe place.
   c. a playground.
   d. a tent.

DAILY Warm-Up 13

Name _____ Date _____

HURRICANES

What kind of storm has an <u>eye</u>? A hurricane!

A hurricane is a big storm. It gets heat and energy from warm water in the ocean. This makes a strong wind.

Hurricanes spin around an eye. It is the center. It is calm and quiet. But watch out! The wind will start again.

Hurricanes bring a lot of rain and big waves. Sometimes, they flood streets and houses. They rip down trees.

Stay inside if there is a hurricane. Stay away from glass. Get ready to leave if the police ask you to!

STORY QUESTIONS

1. In this story, *eye* means . . .
   a. watch something.
   b. something on your face.
   c. a hurricane.
   d. the center of a hurricane.

2. Hurricanes get energy from . . .
   a. houses.
   b. the ocean.
   c. the storm.
   d. their eyes.

3. Hurricanes bring . . .
   a. earthquakes.
   b. tornadoes.
   c. big waves.
   d. big trees.

4. In a hurricane, you should . . .
   a. stay inside.
   b. stay outside.
   c. go surfing.
   d. sit by a window.

Name _____ Date _____

TSUNAMI

"Surf's up!" You might want to say this in a tsunami. This is not a good thing.

Earthquakes and volcanoes can happen under the sea. They cause a tsunami. Then, ocean waves get very big. A tsunami is not just one <u>wave</u>. It is many waves. They can move as fast as 450 miles per hour.

These waves can hit land. Then, houses and stores are smashed. People and animals are hurt.

If you live near the ocean, be aware. If there is an earthquake, wait until it is safe. Then, move to high ground. You don't want to surf these waves!

STORY QUESTIONS

1. Tsunamis happen because of . . .
a. tornadoes.
b. rocks.
c. earthquakes.
d. fire.

2. A tsunami is . . .
a. one small wave.
b. one big wave.
c. many big waves.
d. many small waves.

3. In this story, *wave* means . . .
a. water.
b. bye-bye.
c. squiggly line.
d. surfboard.

4. What should you do before a tsunami?
a. surf
b. swim
c. float
d. move to high ground

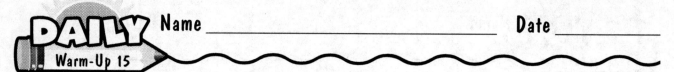

Name _____ Date _____

BLIZZARDS

Snow is pretty. It is fun to play in snow. But too much snow can cause a blizzard.

Cold and strong wind makes a blizzard. A lot of snow falls or blows. Sometimes, you can't see in front of you!

Blizzards can last for hours. They can shut off your power. Make sure you have a flashlight and a radio with a battery.

In a blizzard, go home. Stay inside and stay warm. If you can't get inside, build a snow cave. Never eat snow in a blizzard. It will make you even colder!

STORY QUESTIONS

1. A blizzard is caused by . . .
   a. wind and rain.
   b. cold and waves.
   c. cold and wind.
   d. wind and waves.

2. In a blizzard, you would wear . . .
   a. pants, a coat, and a hat.
   b. pants and a T-shirt.
   c. a T-shirt and a warm hat.
   d. a bathing suit.

3. In a blizzard, make sure you have a . . .
   a. flashlight.
   b. snowboard.
   c. sled.
   d. snowball.

4. If you eat snow in a blizzard, you will get . . .
   a. warmer.
   b. hungry.
   c. colder.
   d. sleepy.

SUN, EARTH, AND MOON

The sun comes up in the morning. The sun goes down at night. This is because Earth spins on its axis.

It takes Earth one day—twenty-four hours—to spin once on its axis. When we see sunlight, our part of Earth faces the sun. When it is dark, we are facing away from the sun.

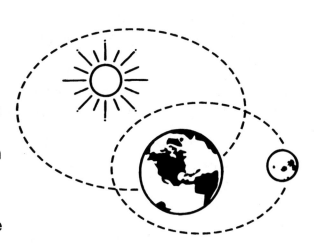

The moon revolves around our Earth. The sun is bright, so we don't always see the moon in the day. But sometimes, we can see the moon and the sun in the same sky.

Earth follows a big circle around the sun. It takes Earth a year to go all the way around the sun. It is a long trip of 365 days!

STORY QUESTIONS

1. Earth revolves around the . . .

a. moon.

b. sun.

c. Earth.

d. morning.

2. There are twenty-four hours in a . . .

a. month.

b. year.

c. day.

d. week.

3. The moon is hidden in the day because . . .

a. Earth is bright.

b. it is shy.

c. it is too cold.

d. the sun is bright.

4. Earth circles the sun in . . .

a. a day.

b. 2 years.

c. 365 days.

d. 24 hours.

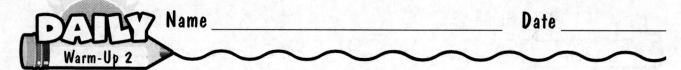

Nonfiction: Science

Name _____   Date _____

FOSSILS

What is a fossil? A fossil is what is left from a very old animal or plant. The word *fossil* means "dug up."

Fossils can be bones. They can also be shapes of bones or plants left in a rock. People dig up rocks. They hope to find clues to our past.

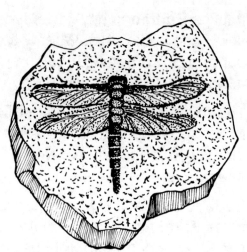

We learn about dinosaurs from fossils. These animals are gone. But they left their bones and shapes behind.

An animal or plant dies. It is buried. Over the years, it breaks down. What is left behind is stone. This is called a fossil.

We can learn a lot from fossils. We learn about our land. We learn about animals. Do you want a fossil? Go digging!

STORY QUESTIONS

1. The word *fossil* means . . .
   a. dig it.
   b. dinosaur.
   c. dug up.
   d. land.

2. Why do people dig up rocks?
   a. to find clues to our past
   b. to hit each other
   c. to hit dinosaurs
   d. to find gold

3. What did dinosaurs leave behind?
   a. babies
   b. bones
   c. sand
   d. plants

4. What should you do if you want a fossil?
   a. dig it up
   b. steal one
   c. make one
   d. bury a plant

DAILY Warm-Up 3 **Name** _____ **Date** _____

WORMS

There are 2,700 kinds of worms. They may be slimy, but they help the earth.

Worms have lived for 120 million years. They eat leaves, stems, and dead roots. Then, their bodies get rid of this matter. This makes rich soil.

One kind of worm from South America is eight feet long. Other worms are only a few inches long. They all dig tunnels and look for food.

If there were no worms, we would be in trouble. Dead animals and plants would pile up. Our dirt would not be good. So if you see a worm, tell it, "Thank you!"

STORY QUESTIONS

1. Worms help the earth by . . .
   a. being slimy.
   b. eating dirt.
   c. eating dead plants and animals.
   d. piling up dead plants and animals.

2. Worms have lived for . . .
   a. 20 million years
   b. 120 million years.
   c. 20 years.
   d. 120 years.

3. Eight-foot long worms live in . . .
   a. America.
   b. North America.
   c. South America.
   d. South Africa.

4. What would happen if we didn't have worms?
   a. Dead plants and animals would pile up.
   b. We would live in tunnels.
   c. We would say, "Thank you!"
   d. We would eat dirt.

DAILY
Warm-Up 4

Name _____   Date _____

TREES

Trees are our friends. We can climb them, and they give us fruit. Best of all, they help us breathe.

We breathe in oxygen and breathe out carbon dioxide. Tree leaves take in carbon dioxide. Then, they make oxygen. We need trees to breathe.

Some trees are 3,000 years old. Some give us apples and pears. They make the air smell good, and they also give us <u>shade</u>.

Would you like to plant a tree? Find some soft dirt. Plant an acorn, and water it every week. Then, you will have your own tree!

STORY QUESTIONS

1. Trees give us . . .
   a. carbon dioxide.
   b. dirt.
   c. water.
   d. fruit.

2. The leaves on trees make . . .
   a. pears.
   b. oxygen.
   c. seeds.
   d. carbon dioxide.

3. In this story, *shade* means . . .
   a. sunglasses.
   b. curtains.
   c. shelter.
   d. color.

4. To grow, a tree seed needs . . .
   a. dirt and water.
   b. acorns.
   c. pears and apples.
   d. 3,000 years.

LIGHTNING

A bolt of lightning can be pretty. It can be scary. It can cause fires. It can also help plants to grow.

Lightning is a big charge of electricity. It shoots down from storm clouds. There are thousands of lightning strikes every day.

These strikes are strong enough to hurt people and destroy things. Lightning can set grass and houses on fire, too.

Plants need nitrogen to grow. Lightning puts nitrogen into the dirt. This helps to keep plants healthy.

In a storm, it is best to stay inside and away from windows and water. Lightning can also strike through the phone. So stay off the phone and stay safely indoors.

STORY QUESTIONS

1. A bolt of lightning can cause . . .

a. water.

b. grass.

c. storms.

d. fires.

2. Lightning is a big charge of . . .

a. nitrogen.

b. electricity.

c. fire.

d. yellow.

3. To grow, plants need . . .

a. fire.

b. clouds.

c. electricity.

d. nitrogen.

4. Lightning can strike you through . . .

a. plants.

b. fire.

c. phones.

d. flowers.

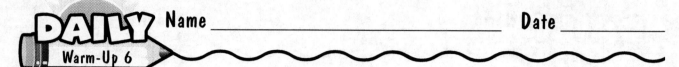

Name _____   Date _____

BUTTERFLY

What looks like a flower that flies through the air? It's a butterfly!

The butterfly is an insect that flies. It starts as an egg. The egg hatches into a caterpillar. It eats many leaves. It eats until it is full.

The caterpillar goes under a leaf. It forms a hard outer shell. It looks like a dead, brown leaf. Inside the shell, it <u>turns into</u> a pretty butterfly! It comes out of the shell ready to fly.

Butterflies have six legs. They drink juice from flowers. They float in the air. Then it is time to lay eggs. The life of a butterfly starts again.

STORY QUESTIONS

1. The butterfly is an insect that . . .
   a. bites.
   b. cries.
   c. flies.
   d. leaves.

2. The caterpillar turns into a . . .
   a. flower.
   b. butterfly.
   c. egg.
   d. leaf.

3. In this story, "turns into" means . . .
   a. becomes.
   b. spins.
   c. twists.
   d. twirls.

4. Butterflies drink . . .
   a. milk.
   b. flowers.
   c. flower juice.
   d. orange juice.

FALL LEAVES

How do leaves know to get ready for winter? Why do they turn red and yellow and orange?

In spring and summer, days are long. Trees make a lot of food, and their leaves are green.

In the <u>fall</u>, the days grow short. There is only a little light, and it is very cold. The trees begin to rest.

The green leaves fade away. Leaves begin to turn red and yellow and orange. Then, they turn brown, and they drop to the ground.

In the spring, it is warm. New leaves appear on the trees, and they are green in color. But we know what will happen to them in the fall!

STORY QUESTIONS

1. Days are long in . . .
   a. spring and fall.
   b. summer and winter.
   c. summer and spring.
   d. fall and winter.

2. In this story, *fall* means . . .
   a. drop.
   b. season.
   c. water.
   d. slip.

3. Trees begin to rest in the . . .
   a. fall.
   b. spring.
   c. summer.
   d. winter.

4. Leaves fall to the ground after . . .
   a. they turn green.
   b. they turn red.
   c. it is spring.
   d. they turn brown.

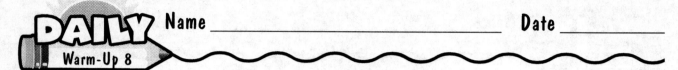

Name _____

Date _____

WHERE ANIMALS GO

In the winter, it is cold and it gets very dark. Animals and birds try to stay warm. They also look for food.

Geese go south in the winter. They fly in a group. They look like a "V." They search for sun and food.

Bears go to sleep for the winter. Their breathing slows down, and they use energy from fat stored in their bodies.

Rabbits do not go to sleep for the winter. Some rabbits grow white fur so they can hide from other animals in the snow. Rabbits eat bark and leaves in the winter.

What do you do in the winter? Do you travel south? Or do you sleep a lot?

STORY QUESTIONS

1. Why do geese fly south?

a. to look for food

b. to look for rabbits

c. to look for birds

d. to go to sleep

2. In the winter, bears . . .

a. fly south.

b. turn white.

c. search for sun.

d. go to sleep.

3. Where do bears get energy in the winter?

a. from rabbits

b. from food

c. from fat

d. from leaves

4. Rabbits grow white fur . . .

a. to sleep.

b. to hide.

c. to eat bark.

d. to look for sun.

STARS

Do you ever wish on the first star at night? Do you sleep under the stars when you go camping? Can you name any stars?

A star is made up of a glowing ball of gas. It is born when a cloud of gas becomes very hot. Some stars are billions of years old. Small stars live longer than big stars.

Our sun is a star. It is the closest star to Earth. It is a medium-sized star.

Most stars occur in groups of two. Big groups of stars are called <u>clusters</u>. A cluster can hold 1,000 stars. That is a lot of wishes!

STORY QUESTIONS

1. Stars are made up of . . .
   a. suns.
   b. clusters.
   c. gas.
   d. wishes.

2. The stars that live the longest are . . .
   a. the biggest.
   b. the brightest.
   c. the smallest.
   d. the sun.

3. The closest star to Earth is . . .
   a. a cluster.
   b. the sun.
   c. the biggest.
   d. the smallest.

4. A cluster is a . . .
   a. big group of stars.
   b. little group of stars.
   c. big group of wishes.
   d. small group of sons.

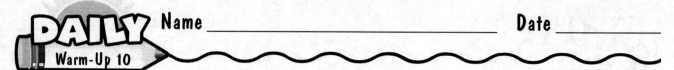

THE MOON

Some nights, the moon is full. Other nights, it is a little slice. Why does the moon change its shape?

The moon makes a circle around Earth. Earth makes a circle around the sun. The moon changes shape when different parts of it are lit up.

When Earth is between the sun and the moon, we see a full moon. We can see just a little of the moon when it is a new moon. This is because the moon is between the sun and Earth.

The moon rises and sets every day. Even if you cannot see it, sometimes the moon is out with the sun during the day!

STORY QUESTIONS

1. The moon makes a circle around . . .

a. stars.

b. Earth.

c. the cloud.

d. the day.

2. A full moon happens when Earth . . .

a. is between the sun and the moon.

b. is between two moons.

c. circles the sun.

d. rises and sets.

3. During a new moon, the moon looks very . . .

a. large.

b. round.

c. little.

d. sunny.

4. What rises and sets every day?

a. the moon and Earth

b. the sun and Earth

c. the moon and the stars

d. the sun and the moon

SHARKS

What fish can only swim forward? It is the same fish you want to watch out for in the ocean. It is a shark!

Sharks have been around since the age of dinosaurs. They live in oceans, and they even live in some rivers and lakes.

Sharks can be small, the size of your hand. They can be big, the size of a bus. Some sharks have 3,000 teeth. When one tooth is lost, they grow another one.

Sharks can only swim forward. Some of them have to keep swimming so they can breathe. Most sharks do not attack people, but some may think you are food and try to bite you.

STORY QUESTIONS

1. Sharks can live in . . .
- a. buses.
- b. swimming pools.
- c. lakes.
- d. fountains.

2. What happens when some sharks lose a tooth?
- a. They swim forward.
- b. They grow another.
- c. They bite you.
- d. They swallow it.

3. Some sharks have to swim forward so they can . . .
- a. bite.
- b. kill.
- c. lose a tooth.
- d. breathe.

4. What is **true** about sharks?
- a. All sharks attack people.
- b. Sharks are all as big as a bus.
- c. Sharks cannot swim backwards.
- d. Sharks can swim backwards.

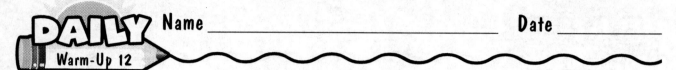

Name _____   Date _____

THE FOOD CHAIN

All animals and plants need food in order to live. They eat each other. This is called the food <u>chain</u>.

A chain is made up of links. Links connect animals and plants. The weakest link in a chain is a plant. This is often eaten by stronger links like deer and horses.

Each link in the food chain is food for the next link. A rabbit eats grass. A coyote eats the rabbit. A cougar eats a coyote. This is the food chain.

People are a link in the food chain, too. The next time you eat a hamburger, think about how it fits into the food chain!

STORY QUESTIONS

1. In order to live, animals and plants need . . .
    a. horses.
    b. hamburgers.
    c. food.
    d. chains.

2. In this story, *chain* means . . .
    a. connection.
    b. necklace.
    c. rope.
    d. daisies.

3. In a food chain, . . .
    a. the weak eat the strong.
    b. rabbits eat cougars.
    c. the strong eat the weak.
    d. cougars eat grass.

4. Which of the following is **true**?
    a. People eat cows.
    b. Cows eat people.
    c. Horses eat cows.
    d. Rabbits eat hamburgers.

Name _____ Date _____

VENUS FLY TRAP

Most plants need water and sunlight to grow. The Venus Fly Trap needs bugs.

The Venus Fly Trap has between four and seven leaves. The edges of these leaves have <u>spikes</u> like little teeth. When the plant feels a bug on its leaves, it closes them up fast!

It takes the Venus Fly Trap ten days to eat a bug. This plant eats only about three bugs in its whole life.

You can buy a Venus Fly Trap for your room! Put it on a sunny windowsill. Water it with rainwater. Then watch it trap bugs!

STORY QUESTIONS

1. The Venus Fly Trap eats . . .

   a. bears.   c. cats.

   b. flies.   d. leaves.

2. In this story, *spikes* mean . . .

   a. sticks.   c. dogs.

   b. spears.   d. teeth.

3. The Venus Fly Trap eats a bug in . . .

   a. ten days.   c. ten years.

   b. ten hours.   d. ten minutes.

4. You should water a Venus Fly Trap with . . .

   a. tap water.

   b. boiling water.

   c. rainwater.

   d. tears.

DAILY
Warm-Up 14

Name _____

Date _____

DUST

What little parts can you find in your bedroom, in your classroom, even in outer space? Dust!

Dust is tiny pieces of matter. You can find it in the air. It can be made up of our old skin. Fibers from our clothes also make up dust.

Dust <u>mites</u> are little bugs. They live in carpets and on beds. They eat dust in our houses. Dust mites can cause an allergy.

Dust lives in outer space, too. Mars has big dust storms. Dust makes up the tails of comets. Dust is everywhere!

STORY QUESTIONS

1. Which statement is **not true**?
   a. Dust is in your classroom.
   b. Dust is on Mars.
   c. Dust is only in California.
   d. Dust is in your carpet.

2. In this story, *mites* mean . . .
   a. strong.
   b. bugs.
   c. carpets.
   d. power.

3. Allergies can be caused by . . .
   a. comets.
   b. outer space.
   c. skin.
   d. dust mites.

4. You can find dust . . .
   a. everywhere.
   b. only on Mars.
   c. nowhere.
   d. only on clothes.

52 ©*Teacher Created Resources, Inc.*

Name _____ Date _____

RAINBOWS

Did you know that light could bend? When it does, it makes a color. This is why we see rainbows!

Some light moves slowly. Some light moves quickly. Every speed of light makes a color. When light moves through rain, it bends. Then, it makes many colors.

Rainbows are made up of red, orange, yellow, green, blue, indigo, and violet. Sometimes, you can even see a double rainbow.

You can not touch a rainbow. It is made up of light and water. But you can enjoy the show!

STORY QUESTIONS

1. When light bends, it makes . . .
   a. water.   c. color.
   b. sun.   d. blue.

2. Light moves at different . . .
   a. speeds.   c. places.
   b. times.   d. rainbows.

3. Rainbows don't show this color—
   a. red.   c. gray.
   b. blue.   d. violet.

4. Rainbows are made up of . . .
   a. light and orange.
   b. speed and sound.
   c. water and show.
   d. light and water.

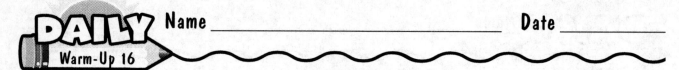

Name _____

Date _____

INVENTIONS

Inventions make our life good. People are smart. They have made things so we are fast, healthy, and happy.

The wheel was invented in the ancient Middle East. Now, we can ride a bike. We can drive a car. The wheel is a good invention.

Inventions make us feel good. Thanks to inventors, we do not get polio. We can get an X-ray. We can even get a new heart.

Some inventions are fun. We can write, and we can hear music. We can take photos, and we can talk on the phone. Let's hear it for inventions!

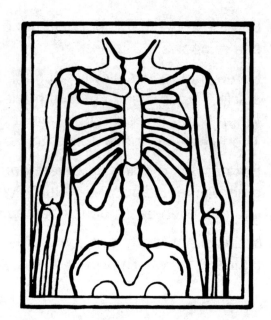

STORY QUESTIONS

1. Inventions make us . . .
    a. slow.   c. sad.
    b. sick.   d. healthy.

2. We can ride a bike because of . . .
    a. X-rays.   c. a new heart.
    b. wheels.   d. music.

3. An *X-ray* is . . .
    a. an invention.   c. from the Middle East.
    b. a new heart.   d. a phone.

4. We can write because someone invented . . .
    a. the wheel.
    b. paper and pencil.
    c. a radio.
    d. a camera.

DAILY
Warm-Up 1

Name _____

Date _____

AMERICAN COLONIES

In 1620, people from England took a boat to America. They decided to live here. They made towns called <u>colonies</u>.

People built homes out of logs from trees. They covered the roof with tree bark. These homes were small. They had a fireplace. They also had a pot for cooking.

The towns were made up of houses. The men hunted for deer and turkey. The women made soap and candles. The children picked berries.

It was hard to live here at first. People were cold and hungry. But they worked hard to make a good home.

STORY QUESTIONS

1. In this story, *colonies* mean . . .
   a. boats.
   b. people.
   c. towns.
   d. England.

2. People cooked over a . . .
   a. stove.
   b. fireplace.
   c. roof.
   d. boat.

3. Children in colonies . . .
   a. hunted deer.
   b. made soap.
   c. picked turkeys.
   d. picked berries.

4. People in colonies were . . .
   a. lazy and slow.
   b. very boring.
   c. always sleeping.
   d. hard-working.

DAILY
Warm-Up 2

Name _____

Date _____

BETSY ROSS

In 1776, Americans did not have a flag. They needed one. Some people think a woman named Betsy Ross made it. She could sew. She had a shop where she stitched cloth onto chairs.

George Washington gave Betsy a picture of a flag. It had seven red stripes. These stripes meant bravery. The flag had six white stripes. They meant truth. The flag had a blue square. Blue meant fairness.

Betsy Ross had never made a flag. But she tried hard. Finally, she made a flag to honor our country. She put in a circle of thirteen stars—one for each colony.

Now our flag has many stars. But it is a lot like the one that Betsy Ross made a long time ago.

STORY QUESTIONS

1. Betsy Ross made a . . .
    a. chair.   c. star.
    b. country.   d. flag.

2. The red stripes on the flag mean . . .
    a. truth.   c. bravery.
    b. fairness.   d. blood.

3. The thirteen stars on Betsy's flag stood for . . .
    a. stripes.   c. truth.
    b. colonies.   d. flags.

4. Our flag today has . . .
    a. more than thirteen stars.
    b. fewer than thirteen stars.
    c. thirteen stars.
    d. Betsy Ross.

THE BALD EAGLE

Did you know that our national bird might have been a turkey? Our leaders wanted a bird to <u>stand</u> for America. Ben Franklin said the turkey would be a good symbol.

Some people wanted the bald eagle. They said that the eagle was brave and strong. They felt that the eagle was free, just like America.

Ben said the bald eagle stole fish from other birds. He said they flew away when small birds fought them. He liked the turkey.

Ben lost the vote. But what if he had won? It would be funny to see a turkey on our money and stamps!

STORY QUESTIONS

1. In this story, *stand* means . . .
   a. on your feet.
   b. be a symbol.
   c. picture holder.
   d. rest.

2. Why did people want the bald eagle as a symbol?
   a. because it is bald
   b. because it is big
   c. because it has feathers
   d. because it is brave

3. Why didn't Ben like the eagle?
   a. It stole fish.
   b. It flew too high.
   c. It was too big.
   d. It had white feathers.

4. The bald eagle is on our . . .
   a. houses.
   b. money and stamps.
   c. turkeys.
   d. books.

DAILY Warm-Up 4 Name _____ Date _____

BISON

Long ago, the bison gave Native Americans food. It gave them clothes, and it gave them houses. They loved this animal.

Native Americans hunted bison, and they ate the meat. They used its <u>hide</u> for clothing. They also made its hide into tents.

The Native Americans did a dance for the bison. They put on clothes to look like the bison. They wanted to bring the bison to their camps.

Then the bison began to die. Now, we are trying to save them. We help them to live on the prairie. They are doing well!

STORY QUESTIONS

1. The bison gave Native Americans . . .
   a. dances.   c. arrows.
   b. prairies.   d. clothes.

2. In this story, *hide* means . . .
   a. cover.   c. bury.
   b. skin.   d. screen.

3. Why did the Native Americans do a dance for the bison?
   a. They wanted the bison to visit them.
   b. They wanted the bison to dance.
   c. They wanted the bison to hide.
   d. They wanted the bison to go away.

4. Where do bison live now?
   a. in tents   c. in camps
   b. on the prairie   d. in the ocean

DAILY Warm-Up 5

Name _____ Date _____

UNCLE SAM

Uncle Sam is a symbol of the United States. He wears a beard, and he has a tall hat. He wears a blue coat. His pants have red and white stripes.

Who is Uncle Sam? Once a man named Sam Wilson worked in a meat plant. He sold meat to the army. He stamped the meat with the letters U.S.

Some people said the letters stood for the United States. Others said they stood for Uncle Sam. The man's name <u>stuck</u>.

Now, people call our government Uncle Sam. They say, "I work for Uncle Sam." The United States has even adopted Uncle Sam as a national symbol!

STORY QUESTIONS

1. Uncle Sam wears . . .
   a. a red coat.   c. checkered pants.
   b. a short hat.   d. a beard.

2. Sam Wilson stamped meat with the letters . . .
   a. S.U.   c. U.S.
   b. S.W.   d. W.S.

3. In this story, *stuck* means . . .
   a. glued.   c. jammed.
   b. stayed.   d. trapped.

4. Uncle Sam is another name for . . .
   a. meat.
   b. striped pants.
   c. the army.
   d. the government.

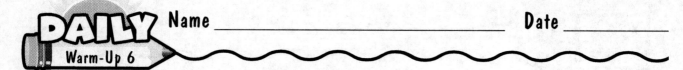

Name _____   **Date** _____

DAILY
Warm-Up 6

YANKEE DOODLE

Do you know the words to the song "Yankee Doodle"? Most kids do. But no one knows who wrote the song!

Once a man from England sang this song. He made fun of soldiers from America. He called them Yankees.

A <u>doodle</u> was a fool. The singer said that Yankees were silly. He said they thought a feather was macaroni. He said that Americans were scared of war cannons. He said they would run home to their mothers.

Then, America had a war with England. North American men sang this song. Bands played it when they won a battle. The song that made fun of us is now one of our most loved tunes!

STORY QUESTIONS

1. Who wrote the words to "Yankee Doodle"?
   a. a Yankee   c. no one knows
   b. a band   d. a mother

2. In this story, *doodle* means . . .
   a. draw.   c. trick.
   b. fool.   d. scribble.

3. The British soldier said Yankees were . . .
   a. silly.   c. smart.
   b. brave.   d. fearless.

4. Who loves the song "Yankee Doodle" now?
   a. mothers
   b. fools
   c. North Americans
   d. no one

DAILY Name _____   Date _____

Warm-Up 7

JOHNNY APPLESEED

Our land has a lot of apple trees. A man named Johnny Appleseed planted some of these trees.

Johnny walked all over the land. Some people say that he walked without any shoes. He wore a tin pot as a hat. He slept on a bed made out of leaves.

All the way, he planted apple seeds. The seeds grew into little trees. Johnny took care of these trees until they grew big. The trees gave people apples.

He loved nature. He gave apple trees to people who were making new homes. Everyone liked him. March 11 is Johnny Appleseed Day. You can plant an apple tree for him!

STORY QUESTIONS

1. How many apple trees did Johnny plant?

a. none   c. some

b. all   d. twenty

2. What did Johnny wear as a hat?

a. a pot   c. an apple

b. leaves   d. nothing

3. What did Johnny give to people?

a. beds   c. homes

b. shoes   d. trees

4. When is Johnny Appleseed Day?

a. May 11

b. March 1

c. March 11

d. in the summer

DAILY Warm-Up 8   Name _____   Date _____

FIREWORKS

What do you do on the Fourth of July? Some kids like to have a picnic. Many people like to set off fireworks.

Fireworks first began in China. They are very old. Later, fireworks went to Europe. Men set them off when they won a war.

Fireworks have bright colors. They can be red and blue and green and white. They can be small. They can be very big. They can be quiet or loud.

Many towns set off fireworks on July 4th. On that day, we won a war against England and became free. Now, we light fireworks as a symbol of winning the battle. But fireworks have hurt kids. Fires have burned down trees. Be careful!

STORY QUESTIONS

1. What do many people do on July 4th?
   a. have a war
   b. light fires
   c. eat fireworks
   d. set off fireworks

2. Fireworks first began in . . .
   a. Europe.
   b. China.
   c. picnics.
   d. England.

3. Fireworks are a symbol of . . .
   a. winning a war.
   b. having a picnic.
   c. red and blue.
   d. burning down trees.

4. Why should you be careful with fireworks?
   a. They start wars.
   b. They are quiet.
   c. They hurt kids.
   d. They are green and white.

DAILY Warm-Up 9   Name _____   Date _____

GEORGE WASHINGTON

George Washington is called the "father of our country." Our capital, Washington, D.C., is named after this man.

George was born in Virginia. He learned to read and write at home. When he was 22, he became a soldier.

Early Americans had to fight to be <u>free</u> from British rule. George led the battle. He was brave and smart. He helped us to win the war.

Then, the people asked George to be the first president of the United States. He helped our country to be brave and free. This is why he is called its father.

STORY QUESTIONS

1. George Washington is called the "father of our country" . . .
   a. because he had children.
   b. because he was our first president.
   c. because he was a soldier.
   d. because he was mean.

2. George studied reading and writing . . .
   a. in Washington, D.C.   c. at home.
   b. in the war.   d. with British soldiers.

3. George helped us to . . .
   a. read and write.   c. lose the war
   b. be soldiers.   d. win the war.

4. In this story, *free* means . . .
   a. independent.   c. no cost.
   b. cheap.   d. fly away.

DAILY Warm-Up 10

Name _____ Date _____

ABE LINCOLN

Abe Lincoln was born in a log cabin. His mother and father did not know how to read or write. He could not go to school very often, so he learned to read and write at home. When he grew up, he became a lawyer.

Abe grew very tall. He was famous for wearing a tall, black hat. He used to keep important papers rolled up in his hat. He worked very hard to help people. He was a very smart man and did not like to see people hurt. He was also very honest and was known by the nickname "Honest Abe."

When Abe was running for president in 1860, an 11-year-old girl named Grace wrote him a letter and told him that his face was too thin. She said that he should grow a beard. And he did! Now when we see pictures of Abraham Lincoln, we usually see him with a beard.

STORY QUESTIONS

1. Abe learned to read and write . . .

   a. at home.

   b. from his mother.

   c. from his father.

   d. at school.

2. Abe used to keep important papers . . .

   a. in his desk at home.

   b. in his pocket.

   c. in his hat.

   d. in his shoe.

3. Abe's nickname was . . .

   a. Good Old Abe.

   b. Honest Abe.

   c. Lawyer Abe.

   d. Happy Abe.

4. An 11-year-old girl told Abe that he should . . .

   a. wear taller shoes.

   b. run for president.

   c. grow a beard.

   d. buy a dog.

DAILY Warm-Up 11 Name _____ Date _____

SACAGAWEA

Sacagawea was a Native American woman. Her name means "bird woman." Like a bird, she was smart. She knew how to live in the wild.

Two men named Lewis and Clark went across the country. Forty men went with them. They wanted to see the Pacific Ocean, but they were hungry and nervous in a new land.

Sacagawea taught them to eat wild plants. She was brave and peaceful. She had a good sense of humor, too.

"Bird Woman" walked with her baby son on her <u>back</u>. She helped Lewis and Clark get to the Pacific Ocean. Now, we have a river and a mountain named for her.

STORY QUESTIONS

1. The name Sacagawea means . . .
   a. "woman who eats birds."   c. "bird woman."
   b. "plant woman."   d. "woman who is smart."

2. How many men went across the country?
   a. 40
   b. 42
   c. 2
   d. 3

3. Sacagawea taught men to . . .
   a. eat wild plants.   c. name rivers.
   b. carry babies.   d. swim.

4. In this story, *back* means . . .
   a. back up.   c. in the past.
   b. reverse.   d. rear.

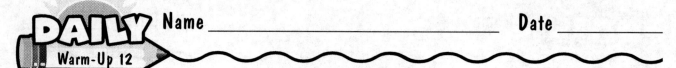

DAILY Warm-Up 12   Name _____   Date _____

HARRIET TUBMAN

Harriet Tubman was a 13-year old girl when she got hurt. She tried to stop a fight between a slave and a master. She believed people should be free.

As an adult, Harriet helped to free her family. Then, she helped other slaves to get free. She walked with them all the way to Canada. On the way, they stopped at houses for food and sleep. These houses were called "safe houses."

Harriet was also a nurse. She took care of men in the Civil War. She also taught newly-freed slaves to live on their own.

Harriet opened a home for old people. She raised money for schools. She also helped women win the <u>right</u> to vote. She was a great woman.

STORY QUESTIONS

1. How did Harriet get hurt?
   a. She raised money for schools.   c. She took care of men in the war.
   b. She walked to Canada.   d. She tried to stop a fight.

2. In "safe houses," slaves could find . . .
   a. traps.   c. schools.
   b. food.   d. enemies.

3. This word that best describes Harriet is . . .
   a. lazy.   c. scared.
   b. caring.   d. bored.

4. In this story, *right* means . . .
   a. hand.
   b. correct.
   c. best.
   d. freedom.

Name _____   Date _____

THE MAYANS

The early Mayan people were smart. They built pyramids and they wrote books. They played games, too.

The Mayans lived in Mexico. They lived in the jungle area. They grew sunflowers and corn. The Mayans called the corn "maize." They prayed to the "maize god" for food.

The Mayans built tall pyramids. They would climb stone stairs to the very top. You can still climb to the top of these pyramids today!

The Mayans wrote books on tree bark and they made art. They also played ball games. Offspring of the Mayans still live in Mexico today.

STORY QUESTIONS

1. In this story, *offspring* means . . .
    a. water.
    b. children.
    c. fountain.
    d. ball games.

2. The Mayans prayed to the . . .
    a. pyramids.
    b. corn god.
    c. tree bark.
    d. jungle.

3. A pyramid is very . . .
    a. tall.
    b. short.
    c. smart.
    d. little.

4. Where can you find Mayans today?
    a. in pyramids
    b. in Mexico
    c. at the ball game
    d. in California

DAILY Name _____ **Date** _____

Warm-Up 14

SPACE TRAVEL

Do you want to travel into space? People want to know what is beyond Earth. They want to see the moon, and they want to see stars. They also want to see Mars!

In July of 1969, the first man walked on the moon. His name was Neil Armstrong. He put a flag on the moon. He said, "That's one small step for man; one giant leap for <u>mankind</u>."

Chimps have traveled into space, too. Dogs and mice and frogs have traveled there. Even insects like ants, spiders, and bees have gone.

Now, we make space shuttles. They can take many people into space. Maybe someday, you will travel to space!

STORY QUESTIONS

1. Why do people want to go into space?
   a. They hate Earth.
   b. They are curious.
   c. They are mean.
   d. They are scared of spiders.

2. In this story, *mankind* means . . .
   a. only men.
   b. only nice men.
   c. all people.
   d. chimps.

3. In July of 1969, . . .
   a. the first man walked on the moon.
   b. the first chimp went into space.
   c. the first chimp put a flag on the moon.
   d. we made space shuttles.

4. What is a space shuttle?
   a. a bus to the Moon
   b. a way to take many people to space
   c. a trolley to Mars
   d. a one-person rocket

DAILY Name _____ Date _____
Warm-Up 1

GERMS

What little living things can make you cough and sneeze and stay in bed for days? Germs!

Germs are so small that you need a microscope to see them. They are found all over the world. They spread when someone sneezes or coughs. Then, they enter our body and make us sick.

Germs produce a <u>toxin</u>. This is like a poison. Some germs cause a fever. Others cause us to be tired. Some cause a rash.

You can protect yourself from germs by washing your hands a lot. Cover your mouth when you cough. Sneeze into the crook of your arm or use a tissue. Then, wash your hands again!

STORY QUESTIONS

1. Which sentence is **true**?

   a. You can see germs on your arm.

   b. Germs are found only in America.

   c. You need a microscope to see germs.

   d. All germs keep us healthy.

2. Some germs are spread by . . .

   a. words.   c. microscopes.

   b. coughs.   d. washing your hands.

3. In this story, the word *toxin* means . . .

   a. coughing.   c. tissue.

   b. sneezing.   d. poison.

4. What should you do after you sneeze?

   a. Wash your hands.   c. Get a microscope.

   b. Go to sleep.   d. Look for germs.

DAILY Name _____ Date _____
Warm-Up 2

EXERCISE

Exercise is any action that gets you moving. You can run, bike, swim, jump rope, or row a boat. It's all good for you!

There are three kinds of exercise. One is stretching. You may do this in dance, yoga, or at the gym. When you stretch, you keep your muscles bendable.

Aerobic exercise makes your heart beat fast. You get this kind of exercise when you walk or run. Your heart beats fast when you swim, too.

The last kind of exercise makes your muscles strong. You build strong muscles when you lift weights.

When you sprint, or run fast, you make your muscles strong, too. You get exercise when you play tag and hide and seek. Leapfrog and ball games are also good to do. So go outside and have fun!

STORY QUESTIONS

1. Exercise is any action that . . .
   a. makes you play tag.
   b. is bad for you.
   c. gets you moving.
   d. is done outside.

2. What happens to your muscles when you stretch?
   a. They beat faster.   c. They break.
   b. They stay bendable.   d. They cry.

3. When you walk or run, your heart . . .
   a. beats faster.   c. stretches.
   b. swims.   d. plays tag.

4. You can build strong muscles by . . .
   a. stretching.   c. sitting on the couch.
   b. eating spinach.   d. lifting weights.

DAILY Warm-Up 3   Name _____   Date _____

HEALTHY FOOD

Healthy food is good for you. You need it for shiny hair and strong bones. You need it so you can grow tall and feel good. The best part about healthy food is that it is tasty!

You can find grains in bread, rice, and oatmeal. You should eat four servings of grains every day. Milk, cheese, and yogurt are also important. These will give you strong bones.

Meat, beans, fish, and nuts give your body iron and protein. You can also eat an egg or some peanut butter to help keep your body healthy. Fruit and vegetables are good to eat. Eat many kinds each week.

Chips and cookies are tasty, but eat only a few at a time. When you eat healthy food, your body will thank you!

STORY QUESTIONS

1. Healthy food will make you . . .

a. sick.

b. strong.

c. green.

d. tasty.

2. What food will help give you strong bones?

a. bread

b. nuts

c. cheese

d. chips

3. What kind of vegetables should you eat each week?

a. none

b. one kind

c. green vegetables

d. many kinds

4. You should eat cookies . . .

a. once in a while.

b. all the time.

c. instead of oatmeal.

d. to grow strong.

DAILY Warm-Up 4 Name _____ **Date** _____

EARS

Your ears are amazing! They help you to hear. They also help to keep you from falling down.

There are three parts to your ear. They are the outer ear, the middle ear, and the inner ear. The outer ear is the part you can see. Its job is to collect sounds, and it also collects earwax.

You can find the eardrum in the middle ear. The eardrum and little bones in your ear help to move sound to your brain. The inner ear has little hairs on it. Sound hits these hairs. Then they move fast to tell the brain what they have heard.

The inner ear is full of fluid. This keeps you from falling down. Ears are amazing. Never poke anything into them, and they will take care of you for life!

STORY QUESTIONS

1. The three parts of the ear are . . .
   a. ear wax, eardrum, and fluid.   c. bones, hairs, and fluid.
   b. outer, middle, and hairy ear.   d. outer, middle, and inner ear.

2. You can find ear wax in the . . .
   a. outer ear.   c. brain.
   b. middle ear.   d. inner ear.

3. The eardrum and little bones help to move sound to your . . .
   a. outer ear.   c. ear wax.
   b. brain.   d. mouth.

4. The inner ear is full of . . .
   a. fluid.
   b. ear wax.
   c. cotton swabs.
   d. bones.

DAILY Warm-Up 5

Name _____ Date _____

LUNGS

What allows you to breathe in fresh air? What allows you to breathe out old air? What allows you to talk? The lungs!

You have two lungs. They take up most of your chest. Your ribs protect your lungs from getting hurt. You can feel your lungs if you put one hand on your chest and breathe deeply.

Your lungs grow big when you breathe in air. Then oxygen from the air goes into your blood. Your body needs oxygen in order to live.

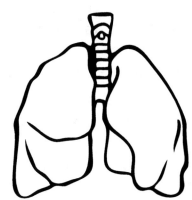

When your body has used up the oxygen it needs, it must get rid of old air. This air is warm from being inside your body. Your lungs breathe it out and make room for new air.

Your lungs help you talk, too. The more air you breathe in, the louder and longer you can talk in one breath. Lungs are important for breathing, talking, and even singing!

STORY QUESTIONS

1. Your ribs . . .
   a. help you to sing.
   b. bring you oxygen.
   c. protect your lungs.
   d. poke your lungs.

2. Oxygen goes from your lungs to your . . .
   a. blood.
   b. ribs.
   c. air.
   d. tongue.

3. Old air is warm because it has been . . .
   a. singing.
   b. inside your bones.
   c. inside your body.
   d. angry.

4. If you take a big breath of air, you can talk . . .
   a. only a short time.
   b. to animals.
   c. loudly.
   d. to your lungs.

DAILY Warm-Up 6

Name _____   Date _____

SLEEP

We all need sleep. Sleep keeps us feeling good, and it keeps the body healthy. How much sleep do you need?

Children need 10 to 12 hours of sleep each night. As you get older, you need about eight hours of sleep each night. Animals, such as cats, sleep about 20 hours a day. They take a lot of naps!

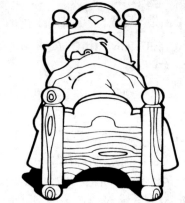

Sleep helps our brains to think well. We can solve problems, and we can be creative. If you didn't sleep, you would get very tired and very sick.

Sleep helps our muscles and bones to repair themselves if they have been hurt. We can fight sickness if we get sleep. Make sure you get exercise at least three hours before bedtime. Your bedroom should be cool, dark, and quiet. Have a good night!

STORY QUESTIONS

1. Children need . . .
   a. 8 hours of sleep each night.
   b. 20 hours of sleep each night.
   c. a lot of naps.
   d. 10 to 12 hours of sleep each night.

2. Sleep allows us to . . .
   a. solve problems and be creative.
   b. think like cats.
   c. get sick.
   d. be very tired.

3. To sleep well, you should exercise . . .
   a. at night.
   b. at least three hours before bedtime.
   c. 20 hours a day.
   d. in the dark.

4. Your bedroom should have . . .
   a. a loud television.
   b. bright lights.
   c. curtains or shades on the windows.
   d. cats.

DAILY Warm-Up 7 | Name _____ Date _____

WATER

Did you know that much of your body is made up of water? If you didn't have water to drink, you would die. Plants and animals must have water, too.

Water doesn't have a smell, and it doesn't have a taste. But we need it because it helps us to be strong. It helps plants to grow, too.

We can find water in many forms. It is in clouds and rain. It is in ice and glaciers. It is in oceans and rivers and lakes. But there are many people on the earth, and some of them don't have much water.

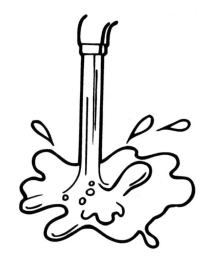

It is good to save water. Turn off the tap water when you wash dishes or brush your teeth. Don't leave the hose <u>running</u>. This way, everyone can enjoy a drink of water.

STORY QUESTIONS

1. We need water to . . .
   a. smell.
   b. live.
   c. die.
   d. taste.

2. What is true about water?
   a. Not everyone has a lot of water.
   b. Everyone has enough water.
   c. No one needs water.
   d. Everyone has a lake.

3. In this story, *running* means . . .
   a. jogging.
   b. racing.
   c. managing.
   d. flowing.

4. You can save water by . . .
   a. leaving on the tap water.
   b. making rain.
   c. turning off the tap water.
   d. washing dishes in the sink.

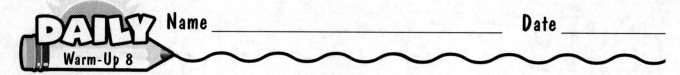

Name _____ **Date** _____

TEETH

You will have 32 of them when you grow up. They are white and shiny, and they help you to eat. They are your teeth, of course!

Babies are not born with teeth. They get them when they are about six months old. Little kids have 20 baby teeth. They fall out when you are about six years old.

Then, you begin to grow adult teeth. They are larger than your baby teeth. They help you to bite into apples and sandwiches. They help you to chew, too.

Make sure to take care of your teeth. <u>Brush</u> your teeth after every meal. Floss between them at least once a day. And don't forget to visit the dentist twice a year. This way, you will always have a bright white smile!

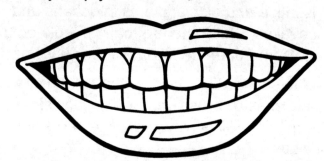

STORY QUESTIONS

1. Adults have . . .
  a. 20 teeth.
  b. 6 teeth.
  c. 32 teeth.
  d. no teeth.

2. Kids lose their baby teeth when they are . . .
  a. six months old.
  b. six years old.
  c. 32 years old.
  d. dentists.

3. Teeth help you to . . .
  a. bite into food.
  b. floss.
  c. grow up.
  d. sleep.

4. In this story, *brush* means . . .
  a. sweep.
  b. touch.
  c. hair.
  d. clean.

Name _____ Date _____

BONES

Without bones, you would not be able to stand. Your skin would fall down, and you could not walk or run. We need our bones!

A baby who has just been born has 300 bones. Slowly, these bones grow and join together. It is important to get plenty of calcium in milk, cheese, and yogurt. Calcium helps your bones to grow strong.

Adults have 206 bones. By the time they are 25 years old, all bones have finished growing. Now, you have a strong skeleton!

Take good care of your bones. For example, wear a helmet when you ride a bike or skate. This will protect your skull. Wear knee pads and elbow pads, too. A broken bone hurts, and it takes a long time to heal. Treat your bones nicely, and they will be nice to you!

STORY QUESTIONS

1. What would happen to your skin without bones?
    a. It would run away.
    b. It would break.
    c. It would fall down.
    d. It would become a skeleton.

2. Babies have . . .
    a. more bones than adults.
    b. no bones.
    c. 206 bones.
    d. fewer bones than adults.

3. In this story, *skeleton* means . . .
    a. a Halloween poster.
    b. a scary thing in a movie.
    c. all of your bones.
    d. dinosaur.

4. A broken bone . . .
    a. helps you ride a bike.
    b. takes a long time to heal.
    c. does not hurt.
    d. protects your skull.

DAILY Warm-Up 10

Name _____

Date _____

COMMON COLD

Are you sneezing and coughing? Do you have a headache? Is your nose running? Is your throat sore? If so, you might have a common <u>cold</u>.

A cold is caused by an infection in the nose. Some colds last for two days, and others last for two weeks. Adults get between two and three colds each year. Children get between six and 10 colds each year!

How do you keep from getting a cold? Wash your hands often. Cold germs can live on doorknobs and other objects. If a sick person opens a door, and then you open a door, you may get a cold. If you touch your nose or eyes, wash your hands right away. If you blow your nose, wash your hands again. This will help to keep colds far away from you!

STORY QUESTIONS

1. If you have a cold, you might get . . .

    a. a broken bone.   c. a doorknob.

    b. a sore throat.   d. spots.

2. A cold is caused by an infection in the . . .

    a. throat.   c. nose.

    b. ear.   d. hands.

3. How can you keep from getting a cold?

    a. blow your nose   c. touch doorknobs

    b. sneeze   d. wash your hands

4. In this story, *cold* means . . .

    a. chilly.

    b. frozen.

    c. illness.

    d. cool.

Name _____   Date _____

CHICKEN POX

Chicken pox has nothing to do with chickens. It is a disease that usually affects kids. But don't worry. Chicken pox will make you itch, but it won't hurt you.

Chicken pox has been around for hundreds of years. If you get it, you will have a fever. You will also have sores on your body. These sores itch!

You can catch chicken pox through the air. This is why it spreads through schools so quickly. It is important to cover your mouth when you cough or sneeze and to wash your hands.

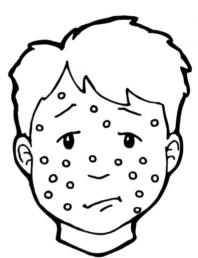

Now you can get a shot to prevent chicken pox. But if you do get this disease, it won't last long. You can take a bath in oatmeal. This will stop the itching!

STORY QUESTIONS

1. Chicken pox usually affects . . .

   a. adults.
   b. chickens.
   c. sores.
   d. kids.

2. What will you get if you have chicken pox?

   a. sores
   b. chickens
   c. oatmeal
   d. broken bones

3. Chicken pox is a disease that spreads through . . .

   a. oatmeal.
   b. the air.
   c. sores.
   d. itching.

4. Why is oatmeal useful to kids with chicken pox?

   a. It is healthy.
   b. It itches.
   c. It stops the itching.
   d. It helps a fever.

DAILY Warm-Up 12

Name _____ Date _____

EYES

Your eyes work hard. From the moment you wake up until you close them in bed at night, they are on duty. It is good to take care of your eyes.

You should use a light when you read. That way, your eyes will not have to work as hard. But too much sunlight is bad for your eyes. Make sure to wear sunglasses when you are out in bright sun.

It hurts to get poked or hit in the eye. When you play hockey or ski, make sure to wear goggles. Don't run with pencils, scissors, or other sharp objects. Be careful of other people's eyes, too.

If you have a hard time seeing, you should get your eyes checked by a doctor. You may need eyeglasses. Treat your eyes well. They work hard for you!

STORY QUESTIONS

1. You should read with . . .
- a. sunglasses.
- b. a light.
- c. goggles.
- d. a doctor.

2. Wear goggles when you play hockey in case . . .
- a. there is bright sun.
- b. your eyes are on duty.
- c. you have a pencil.
- d. you get hit in the eye.

3. You should be careful of . . .
- a. only your eyes.
- b. only other people's eyes.
- c. no one's eyes.
- d. everyone's eyes.

4. Where should you go if you have trouble seeing?
- a. to a doctor
- b. to a hockey game
- c. skiing
- d. to bed

DAILY Name _____ Date _____
Warm-Up 13

GETTING MAD

Getting mad is normal. We get mad if a friend hurts us. We get mad if a toy breaks. But it is good to control your anger so you don't hurt yourself or anyone else.

Your heart beats fast when you get mad. Your face might get red. You may want to hit or kick or yell. Everyone feels mad sometimes.

There are good ways to control your anger. Never call someone names or hurt them. Instead, go away by yourself for a few minutes. Take deep breaths. Go for a run if you need to.

Then, say what you <u>feel</u> out loud. You might say, "I feel mad because I broke my doll." You could say, "I feel mad because my friend hurt my feelings." When you are calm, talk about how you feel with friends, teachers, or parents. Think about what you can do to feel better.

STORY QUESTIONS

1. Who gets mad?
   a. everyone
   b. only you
   c. only kids
   d. only parents

2. When you get mad, you should . . .
   a. call someone "stupid."
   b. take deep breaths.
   c. kick your friend.
   d. yell at your dog.

3. In this story, *feel* means . . .
   a. touch.
   b. pet.
   c. hate.
   d. think.

4. Getting mad is . . .
   a. wrong.
   b. silly.
   c. bad.
   d. normal.

DAILY Warm-Up 14

Name _____ Date _____

BRUISES

You bump your arm. You bump it hard. You do not get cut. Your skin does not break. Still, you get a bruise. Your skin turns blue-black. Why does this happen?

Blood flows in your body through tubes. Tubes that carry blood are called blood vessels. You have so many blood vessels in your body. You have enough blood vessels to go around the world! Some tubes are big. Some tubes are tiny.

Living things are made of cells. Cells are like building blocks. They are the smallest building block of living things. Your body has lots of cells. You have bone cells. You have skin cells. You have blood cells, too. You have lots of blood cells. Red blood cells make your blood look red.

When you get bumped, you may hurt some tiny blood vessels. Some may break. You bleed under your skin. When blood cells leak from the tubes, they die. When the cells die, they turn blue-black. We see the blue-black color. We call the blue-black color a bruise.

After many days, the bruise changes color. It changes from blue-black to purple. It changes from purple to yellow. Finally, the bruise is gone.

STORY QUESTIONS

1. This passage is mainly about . . .
   a. cells
   b. bruises
   c. blood
   d. colors

2. What are living things made of?
   a. blood
   b. vessels
   c. cells
   d. tubes

3. If your bruise is yellow, it means that . . .
   a. soon the bruise will be gone.
   b. you are bleeding under the skin.
   c. it will always stay that way.
   d. soon the bruise will be purple.

4. Which statement is **true**?
   a. You do not have bone cells.
   b. You do not have many blood vessels.
   c. When you get a bruise, you cut your skin.
   d. Red blood cells make your blood look red.

DAILY Warm-Up 15

Name _____ Date _____

LAUGHTER

Ha, ha, ha! The average person laughs 17 times a day. When is the last time you laughed? Laughing is good for your body and brain!

When you laugh, your mouth opens. You smile, and you take in more air, which gives more oxygen to the brain. You make funny noises, and the beat of your heart speeds up. Best of all, you feel happy. Laughing can calm you down if you are feeling angry.

It is fun to laugh with people. We laugh at jokes, and we laugh at TV shows. We laugh at movies, at clowns, and at the funny things that animals do.

Some scientists say that dogs can laugh, too. They make a sound like <u>panting</u> when they are happy. What does your own laugh sound like?

STORY QUESTIONS

1. The average person laughs . . .
 a. all day.
 b. 7 times a day.
 c. with people.
 d. 17 times a day.

2. What do you take in when you laugh?
 a. bugs
 b. air
 c. clowns
 d. dogs

3. Who says dogs can laugh?
 a. other dogs
 b. the average person
 c. some scientists
 b. clowns

4. In this story, *panting* means . . .
 a. clothes.
 b. shorts.
 c. breathing quickly and loudly.
 d. telling a joke.

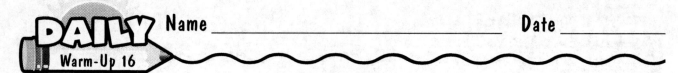

Name _____ **Date** _____

Warm-Up 16

ALLERGIES

Does your skin swell and itch after a bee sting? When you eat peanuts, do you have trouble taking a breath? Do your eyes <u>burn</u> in the spring? If so, you might have allergies.

An allergy means that something in the air or in your food makes you sick. You might eat a peanut butter cookie and be happy. But your friend could feel sick after eating the same cookie. Your sister might feel fine after a bee sting, but you might get a rash and feel bad.

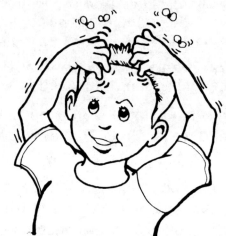

Some kids are allergic to dogs or cats. Some get sick when trees or flowers bloom. It is good to know what makes you sick. Then, you can stay away from it. Your doctor can test you. This way, you will stay happy and feeling good.

STORY QUESTIONS

1. If you are allergic to bees, a sting might give you . . .
- a. a cookie.
- b. a cat.
- c. a rash.
- d. a flower.

2. In this story, *burn* means . . .
- a. flames.
- b. hurt.
- c. fire.
- d. candle.

3. If you feel sick after eating a peanut, you could have . . .
- a. an allergy.
- b. a dog.
- c. a sandwich.
- d. a cookie.

4. If something makes you sick, you should . . .
- a. eat more.
- b. get a cat.
- c. get mad.
- d. get tested.

FOODS WITH COLOR

Red berries. Orange carrots. Green peppers. Fruits and vegetables come in many colors. The more colors you eat, the better you will feel!

Eat your greens. Broccoli, spinach, and dark green lettuce are good for you. You can make a salad or a tasty stir-fry dish. Eat your blues, too. Blueberries and grapes will keep your body well.

Red foods like tomatoes are good. So are orange foods like oranges and carrots. Don't forget yellow foods! Bananas are not only for monkeys. They will keep you healthy, too.

Every day, your plate can be full of color. Try to see how many colors you can eat at every meal.

STORY QUESTIONS

1. If you eat many colors, you will feel . . .
- a. sick.
- b. rainbows.
- c. healthy.
- d. blue.

2. You can make a salad out of . . .
- a. spinach.
- b. monkeys.
- c. crayons.
- d. yellow.

3. Grapes will keep your body . . .
- a. full.
- b. sick.
- c. blue.
- d. well.

4. Every day, your plate should be full of . . .
- a. color.
- b. monkeys.
- c. dessert.
- d. cake.

DAILY Name _____ **Date** _____
Warm-Up 18

TALK IT OUT

Did your dog eat your good pair of shoes? Did your friend move away? Did your little brother break your game? Bad things happen to everyone. It is good to learn how to deal with them.

Some people keep their feelings <u>inside</u>. They may feel sad. They may feel mad. They don't let anyone know. This may make them feel sick. They may not sleep.

It is important to talk about your problems. You might want to talk to your parent. You might want to talk to your teacher. Maybe you have a good friend to talk with. Maybe you would feel best talking to a doctor.

When you talk about a problem, people can help you to work it out. You will see that things are not as bad as you thought. You will feel better. The next time something goes wrong, you may even be able to laugh about it!

STORY QUESTIONS

1. When you have a problem, you should . . .
  a. keep it inside.
  b. talk it out.
  c. get sick.
  d. sleep poorly.

2. In this story, *inside* means . . .
  a. in the house.
  b. in the classroom.
  c. in your body and brain.
  d. in your refrigerator.

3. When you talk about a problem, . . .
  a. people can help you.
  b. people will laugh at you.
  c. the doctor will give you a shot.
  d. you will get sick.

4. Sometimes, bad things happen to . . .
  a. little brothers.
  b. doctors.
  c. teachers.
  d. everyone.

FICTION

Contemporary
Realistic Fiction

Mystery/Suspense/Adventure

Historical
Fiction

Fantasy

Fairy Tales/Folklore

88 ©Teacher Created Resources, Inc.

DAILY ~Name~ _____ **Date** _____

Warm-Up 1

THE FARMER'S CORN

Farmer Fran liked to share the corn that she grew on her farm. She gave her neighbors corn on the cob. She also gave them <u>kernels</u> so that they could plant their own corn.

"You grow the best corn in the whole world," Farmer Fred said to her. "Why do you give away kernels? You should keep them all for yourself."

Farmer Fran laughed. Then she said, "Corn has a powder called pollen. It needs pollen from other corn stalks in order to grow well. Pollen travels on the wind."

"So?" Farmer Fred said.

"So," Farmer Fran continued. "If my neighbors grow good corn, their pollen will travel on the wind to my corn. It will make my corn better. Then we can all grow the best corn in the world!"

STORY QUESTIONS

1. In this story, *kernels* mean . . .
    a. wind.
    b. seeds.
    c. farmers.
    d. cakes.

2. What powder helps corn to grow well?
    a. kernels
    b. stalks
    c. pollen
    d. wind

3. How does pollen travel?
    a. in the wind
    b. in a boat
    c. in the dirt
    d. on a shovel

4. Why does Farmer Fran give away corn kernels?
    a. because she is mean
    b. because she is silly
    c. because they are bad
    d. because they make her corn better

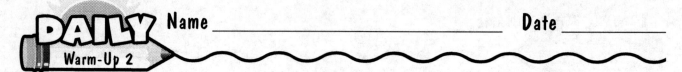

THE FISHERWOMAN

There was once a fisherwoman named Laura. She fished better than anyone in her town. Every day, she took her boat out onto the sea. Every night, she brought home fish for the people in her town to eat. "She is such a kind woman!" they cried.

One day, Laura took her boat out to sea. It had been sunny, but now the fog blew in. Rain hit Laura's boat. The waves grew <u>rough</u>. Laura tried to steer her boat, but the wind was too strong. Her boat tipped over. Laura fell into the cold dark water.

The ocean spirit smiled. He would help this woman who was so good to her friends. He raised Laura up on his waves and carried her to shore. When the people in town saw Laura safe on the sand, they cheered. Then, they wrapped her in their own coats and fed her bowls of soup. "We are glad that now we can give something to you," they said.

STORY QUESTIONS

1. Why do people love Laura?

   a. because she is a good fisherwoman

   b. because she has a boat

   c. because she is so kind

   d. because she needs help

2. In this story, *rough* means . . .

   a. mean.   c. sandpaper.

   b. choppy.   d. bully.

3. Why does the ocean spirit help Laura?

   a. because she likes fish   c. because she needs soup

   b. because she has a boat   d. because she is good to her friends

4. What do the people give Laura?

   a. a new boat   c. soup

   b. her coat   d. a fish

     ©*Teacher Created Resources, Inc.*

DAILY Name _____ **Date** _____

Warm-Up 3

TALKING TREES

A long time ago, a girl named Julie lived in the woods. Her mother and father built a little log house from trees that had fallen down. Julie played all day with deer and rabbits. At night, she and her parents ate dinner in the warm cabin.

Julie had a good life, but she was lonely. She leaned her head against a tall oak tree. "I wish I had a friend," she said.

A bright light flashed, and a pretty woman stepped out of the oak. "I am the fairy of the tree," she said. "Because you are so kind, the trees will talk to you." She touched Julie's head with a branch, and then vanished.

From then on, Julie could hear all the trees talking. She learned their names. She learned how to care for them. The trees became her friends, and she was never lonely again.

STORY QUESTIONS

1. Julie's parents build a house out of . . .
    a. rabbits.
    b. oaks.
    c. fallen trees.
    d. fairies.

2. Why is Julie lonely?
    a. She misses her rabbits.
    b. She has no friends.
    c. The trees can talk.
    d. She lives in a log house.

3. The fairy allows Julie to . . .
    a. hear the trees talking.
    b. hear the trees crying.
    c. hear deer talking.
    d. fly away.

4. What does Julie learn about the trees?
    a. She learns that they hit her.
    b. She learns that they don't like her.
    c. She learns that they are lonely.
    d. She learns their names and how to care for them.

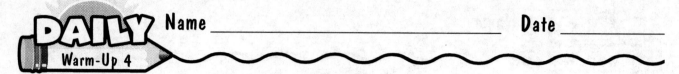

THE SHARING MAN

Once, there lived an old man who had no money. He ate what he found on the land. He shared his food with the animals and birds around him.

One winter, he sat with his head in his hands. "I can't find any food on the land," he cried. "The mushrooms are gone. The dandelions and berries are gone. I will starve."

But the Forest Fairy heard his cry. She spoke to the squirrels and birds. "Your friend needs your help now," she said.

The squirrels brought nuts from hiding places in the trees. The birds brought dried berries from hiding places in the ground. "Here," they said to the man. "Share our food."

The foxes curled up to warm the old man's feet, and the deer nestled beside him. The man ate the nuts and berries, warm and happy with his friends.

STORY QUESTIONS

1. What does the old man share with animals and birds?
    a. his money   c. his house
    b. his food   b. his bed

2. In winter, the man is afraid he will . . .
    a. cry.   c. starve.
    b. share.   d. laugh.

3. The squirrels hide . . .
    a. nuts.   c. mushrooms.
    b. berries.   d. dandelions.

4. Why do the animals and birds help the old man?
    a. because he is mean
    b. because he helps them
    c. because the Forest Fairy makes them
    d. because they don't like him

Name _____   **Date** _____

THE ROYAL WEDDING

The handsome Prince Tulip wanted a wife. He looked in the garden for a lady that was good and kind. Finally, he found Daisy. She loved to water flowers. She fed birds from her hands. She played the harp for spiders and ants.

"Will you marry me?" Prince Tulip asked Daisy.

"Yes," she said. They chose a wedding day and met beneath the roses. The flowers dropped petals upon their heads. Birds brought them nuts and berries. Just as Prince Tulip was about to kiss his bride, she held up her hand. "Stop!" she cried. "We don't have a ring."

The spiders whispered to each other. They spun a ring of fine, strong silk. Then, the ants carried it to Prince Tulip. He slipped the ring on Daisy's finger. From then on, when it rained, Daisy's ring sparkled like diamonds.

STORY QUESTIONS

1. Prince Tulip wants a wife who is . . .
   - a. beautiful.
   - b. mean.
   - c. kind.
   - d. rich.

2. What do the birds bring to Tulip and Daisy?
   - a. a ring
   - b. spider webs
   - c. a harp
   - d. berries

3. Why does Daisy cry "Stop!"?
   - a. She doesn't have a ring.
   - b. She doesn't have a harp.
   - c. She doesn't like flower petals.
   - d. She wants real diamonds.

4. Who makes Daisy's ring?
   - a. spiders
   - b. ants
   - c. birds
   - d. Prince Tulip

Name _____

Date _____

THE STRONG PRINCESS

Once upon a time, there lived a strong princess. She could build castle walls with heavy rocks. She could put fallen trees across the river to make a bridge. She could even pick up her horse!

The boys in the land thought they should be stronger than a girl. "People will think we're weak if the princess can lift more than we can," they said. They decided to trick the princess.

One day, she walked on the road with her horse and saw an awful <u>sight</u>. Two boys lay under a fallen tree in the mud. The princess tried to lift the tree. She tried and she tried, but she could not lift it. She fell in the mud. The boys jumped up. "You're not strong now," they laughed.

The princess saw what had happened. The boys had tied a rope around the tree and weighted it down with a big rock. But the princess said nothing. She knew that she was strong. That was all that mattered.

STORY QUESTIONS

1. Why were the boys in the land unhappy?
 a. The princess could pick up a horse.
 b. The princess laughed and laughed.
 c. The princess was a girl.
 d. The princess was stronger than they were.

2. In this story, *sight* means . . .
 a. eye.
 b. scene.
 c. glasses.
 d. see.

3. Why couldn't the princess lift the tree?
 a. The boys had weighted it down.
 b. She was weak.
 c. She was afraid.
 d. She said nothing.

4. What is **true** about the princess?
 a. She plays tricks on people.
 b. She brags a lot.
 c. She knows her strengths.
 d. She is mean to boys.

©Teacher Created Resources, Inc.

DAILY Name _____ **Date** _____

Warm-Up 7

KING CHEESE

Once, there lived a mouse named King Cheese who ruled the land. He visited each mouse house to make sure all the mice were well. On his trips, he forgot to pack food. So he got very hungry. "Oh, I wish that all I touched would turn to cheese!" he said.

A yellow fairy appeared and said, "Your wish has been granted!" King Cheese reached for his sword. It turned into cheese. He knocked on a door. The door turned to cheese. A mouse bit a hole in the door and stepped out. "Your majesty?" The king shook the mouse's hand. The mouse turned to cheese, too. "Help! Help!" cried the king. But everything he touched turned to cheese. He sat down and cried big, cheesy tears. "I'm sorry! I will always pack food before a trip!" he said.

At once, cheese turned back into houses and grass and mice. From that day on, King Cheese always carried a little bag of cheese on his trips. He never got hungry again.

STORY QUESTIONS

1. Why is King Cheese always hungry?
   a. because he goes on trips   c. because he loves cheese
   b. because he forgets to take food d. because he rules the land

2. What happens to the king's sword?
   a. It turns into a fairy.   c. It turns into cheese.
   b. It turns into a mouse.   d. It cuts the king.

3. Why does the king cry for help?
   a. because everything has turned to cheese
   b. because he is hungry
   c. because he sees a fairy
   d. because he packs food for his trip

4. What is the message of the story?
   a. Be prepared.   c. Watch out for fairies.
   b. Eat cheese.   d. Cry for help.

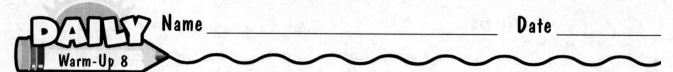

DAILY Warm-Up 8

Name _____ Date _____

PAUL BUNYAN'S DINNER

Paul Bunyan had arms the size of tree trunks. His chest was as big as a house. For dinner, he liked to eat a hundred hamburgers. He drank fifty buckets of milk.

One day, the river flooded. "Help! Help!" cried the people of the town.

Paul heard them. He picked up the whole town and moved it to the top of a mountain.

The people were happy. They wanted to cook Paul dinner to thank him. They cooked and cooked. They put twenty tables together on the grass. They covered the tables with food.

When Paul walked up, the tables were so heavy with food that they broke. "That's okay," Paul said. He sat on the ground and picked up a hamburger. "We'll just have a big picnic on the grass!"

STORY QUESTIONS

1. In this story, Paul is . . .
   a. a small man.
   b. not very hungry.
   c. weak.
   d. big and strong.

2. What does Paul do to the town?
   a. He throws it in the river.
   b. He cooks dinner.
   c. He moves it.
   d. He throws it down the river.

3. Why do the people want to cook for Paul?
   a. to thank him
   b. to punish him
   c. to starve him
   d. because they are afraid

4. Why do the tables break?
   a. They are covered with food.
   b. They are on the grass.
   c. There is a flood.
   d. Paul sits on them.

DAILY
Warm-Up 9

Name _____ Date _____

PRINCE PETER'S PEAS

Prince Peter did not like to eat his peas. He always threw them on the floor. "Please, Peter," the Queen begged. "Eat your peas because they will keep you healthy."

"Eat your peas, son," the King said. "I am tired of stepping on them."

The King tried to hide peas in mashed potatoes. Prince Peter found them. He spit out the peas, one by one.

The Queen hid peas in a stew. Prince Peter picked out the peas and put them in a potted plant.

"What will we do?" the King and Queen asked. Then, the Queen had an idea. She put peas in a blender. She put in milk and ice cream in the blender, too. Then, she mixed it all up.

"A green milkshake?" said Prince Peter. He tasted it. "That is good!" He drank the whole thing. The Queen and King looked at each other and smiled.

STORY QUESTIONS

1. What does Prince Peter do with his peas?
   a. He eats them with potatoes.   c. He hides them in a stew.
   b. He puts them into a milkshake.   d. He throws them on the floor.

2. The King wants Peter to eat his peas because . . .
   a. he is tired of stepping on them.
   b. he wants his son to grow strong.
   c. peas are bad for you.
   d. he has a good idea.

3. Why is the milkshake green?
   a. The Queen put potatoes in it.   c. The Queen put peas in it.
   b. The King put peas in it.   d. The King put a plant in it.

4. What does Prince Peter think of the milkshake?
   a. He hates it.   c. He thinks it tastes good.
   b. He puts it in a plant.   d. He throws it on the floor.

Name _____

Date _____

VULCAN'S FIRE

Everyone was afraid of Vulcan. He loved to play with fire, and he was not safe. "He will burn us and all of our things," said his brothers.

"He will burn up our house," said his sisters.

One day, Vulcan played with a candle. He dipped his finger in the hot wax. "Ouch, that burns!" he said.

"Do not play with fire!" his father said. But Vulcan didn't listen. He leaned in too close to the candle. His hair caught on fire. Even his eyebrows burned. His brothers threw water on him, but it was too late. Vulcan was bald. He had no eyebrows.

"We told you not to play with fire," his sisters said. Then Vulcan threw away his matches and his candle. From then on, he only played in the lake where there was no fire. And no one was afraid of him any more.

STORY QUESTIONS

1. Why are people afraid of Vulcan?
    a. because he is bald
    b. because he plays with fire
    c. because he has no eyebrows
    d. because he plays in the lake

2. What happens when Vulcan plays with the candle?
    a. He burns up the house.
    b. He burns up his brothers.
    c. His sisters throw water on him.
    d. His hair catches on fire.

3. What happens to Vulcan's eyebrows?
    a. They get wet.
    b. They burn off.
    c. They get wax on them.
    d. They float away.

4. Why does Vulcan play in the lake?
    a. because he loves fire
    b. because he is bald
    c. because there is no fire
    d. because his sisters are there

DAVY'S HAT

Davy Crockett had a very cold head. "I need a hat to keep my head warm," he said. "I walk outside, and the wind chills my head."

The animals ran over to him and offered to be Davy's new hat. "Pick me! Pick me!" cried Cat.

Davy set Cat on his head. "Ouch!" he said. "Your claws are too sharp."

Bird waved her wing. "Pick me! Pick me!" Davy set Bird on his head. "Brrr!" he cried. "Your feathers do not keep me warm."

Then Davy saw a round bundle of fur. It was asleep by a rock. "Who is that?" he asked the animals.

"That's Raccoon," they said.

Davy picked up Raccoon, and he put him on his head. "Soft and warm," Davy said. "I have found the perfect hat."

Raccoon just yawned and went back to sleep.

STORY QUESTIONS

1. Why does Davy need a hat?

   a. His head is too hot.

   b. He has wings.

   c. He is sleepy.

   d. His head is cold.

2. Who has sharp claws?

   a. Bird

   b. Cat

   c. Davy

   d. Raccoon

3. Who is a round bundle of fur?

   a. Cat

   b. Raccoon

   c. Davy

   d. Bird

4. Why is Raccoon the perfect hat?

   a. because he is soft and warm

   b. because he has sharp claws

   c. because he has feathers

   d. because he is awake

DAILY Warm-Up 12

Name _____ Date _____

ATHENA'S OWL

Athena loved her owl. It went with her all over the palace. It always rode on her shoulder and called "Whoo, whoo!" in her ear. But one day, she could not find her owl.

She went to see Zeus. "Have you seen my owl?" she asked.

Zeus shook his head. "Sorry. Go ask my wife, Hera."

Athena found Hera in the garden. "Have you seen my owl?

"Why, no," said Hera. "Have you looked in the forest?"

Grumbling, Athena walked into the forest. She called for her owl. "Whoo, whoo!" But no one answered.

Then, off in the distance, she heard two voices. "Whoo, whoo! Whoo, whoo!" they called. Athena walked toward the voices. There in a tree sat her owl. Next to him sat another owl.

Athena just laughed. "It's a good thing I have two shoulders," she said. "Let's all go back to the palace."

STORY QUESTIONS

1. Where does Athena's owl ride?
   a. in a car   c. on her shoulder
   b. with Zeus   d. in a tree

2. Who is Zeus's wife?
   a. Hera   c. the owl
   b. Mrs. Zeus   d. Athena

3. Who is with Athena's owl?
   a. Hera   c. another owl
   b. Zeus   d. no one

4. Why is Athena glad to have two shoulders?
   a. because both owls can ride on them
   b. because she can go to the palace
   c. because she is lost
   d. because she is in a tree

BIGFOOT!

Molly and Brent walked along the Oregon Trail. They wanted to make a new home near the sea. Molly walked in front, and Brent walked in back.

"Wow, Molly," said Brent. "You have big footprints."

Molly frowned. "My feet are small," she said.

"No, they are big," Brent said. "Look at that!"

He showed Molly a footprint. It was as big as a wagon wheel! "That is not my footprint," said Molly.

Then, Molly and Brent looked around. They saw large footprints that led to the forest. Something moved in the trees. Then it vanished. "Bigfoot!" cried Molly and Brent. Their voices scared Bigfoot so much that they never saw him again.

STORY QUESTIONS

1. Why do Molly and Brent walk on the Oregon Trail?
   a. They are looking for Bigfoot.   c. They like to hike.
   b. Molly has big feet.   d. They want to make a new home.

2. Who has small feet?
   a. Brent   c. Bigfoot
   b. Molly   d. everyone

3. What do Molly and Brent see?
   a. small footprints   c. large footprints
   b. berries   d. ghosts

4. Why does Bigfoot vanish?
   a. because he is scared
   b. because he doesn't like the sea
   c. because he has big feet
   d. because he is mean

DAILY
Warm-Up 14

Name _____

Date _____

ANNIE'S CAT

Annie Oakley was excellent at rope tricks. She could rope a cow from twenty feet away, and she could rope a snake in the grass. She could even rope her baby brother.

"I'll bet you a dollar you can't rope a cat," said her friend Wild Bill.

"I'll bet you I can," said Annie.

So Wild Bill found Annie a cat. It was a big brown cat, and it was wild. It ran up a tree, and it chased its tail.

Annie threw her rope. It missed the cat. She threw it again. The cat ran off and chased a butterfly. Annie thought hard. Finally, she put down her rope. "Here, kitty, kitty," she called.

The cat ran over to her. Annie put the rope gently around its back. "Meet my new pet cat," she told Wild Bill. "I'll use your dollar to buy cat food!"

STORY QUESTIONS

1. Annie is good at . . .
   a. climbing trees.
   b. chasing cats.
   c. rope tricks.
   d. cat tricks.

2. Wild Bill finds Annie a big, brown . . .
   a. cat.
   b. tree.
   c. rope.
   d. dollar.

3. What happens when Annie tries to rope the cat?
   a. It climbs a tree.
   b. It chases a butterfly.
   c. It scratches Wild Bill.
   d. It runs to her.

4. What will Annie buy with her dollar?
   a. a new cat
   b. a new rope
   c. food for Bill
   d. cat food

DAILY Name _____ **Date** _____

Warm-Up 15

LOOKING FOR A HEAD

The Headless Horseman could not find his head. "Now where did I put it?" he said to himself. "Is this it?"

He picked up a cabbage and put it on his neck. But when he leaned down to tie his shoes, the rabbits ate the cabbage.

He picked up a basketball. "Maybe this is my head." He put it on his neck. But a tall girl took the basketball and tossed it through a hoop.

"The problem is that I need eyes," he said to his sister.

Then, she put a potato on his neck. "This has eyes," she said.

The Headless Horseman blinked his eyes. He looked in the mirror. "This is a potato," he said. Then he spotted something under the bed. "My head!" he cried. He put his head back on his neck, and his sister cooked the potato for his dinner.

STORY QUESTIONS

1. What happens to the cabbage?
   a. His sister cooks it.
   b. A girl tosses it through a hoop.
   c. It blinks.
   d. The rabbits eat it.

2. Who tosses the basketball?
   a. the Headless Horseman   c. his sister
   b. a tall girl   d. a tall boy

3. Where is the Headless Horseman's head?
   a. under the bed   c. in a field
   b. in the oven   d. on the basketball court

4. What does the Headless Horseman have for dinner?
   a. a horse   c. a cabbage
   b. a potato   d. a basketball

DAILY Warm-Up 1

Name _____ Date _____

THE UGLY BOY

Abe was taller than any kid his age. He had long, bony fingers, and he had a big nose and big ears. "You're ugly!" the other kids cried.

Abe looked in the mirror. He felt sad, because he did not look like the other boys. "I am ugly," he said. "No one will ever love me."

As he grew older, Abe read book after book. He learned about the world. Finally, he asked a pretty woman named Mary to be his wife. She knew how smart Abe was. "I will marry you," she said.

Then, Abe became president of the United States. He was a good and kind man. People liked his big nose and ears. Artists wanted to sculpt his face out of clay. They wanted to paint him. All over the country, people loved Abe Lincoln.

STORY QUESTIONS

1. Why did kids make fun of Abe?
   a. because he was president
   b. because he had a big nose
   c. because he read a lot
   d. because he got married

2. As he grew older, Abe grew . . .
   a. ugly.
   b. sad.
   c. smart.
   d. silly.

3. Why did artists want to sculpt Abe Lincoln?
   a. because they loved him
   b. because he was ugly
   c. because he was mean
   d. because he read books

4. From this story, we learn that . . .
   a. people like big noses.
   b. ugly people should give up.
   c. people love art.
   d. we love people who are good and kind.

DAILY Name _____ **Date** _____

Warm-Up 2

QUENTIN'S PONY

Archie Roosevelt felt ill. "My head hurts, and I'm tired," he told his mother.

"Go to bed and rest," she said.

Archie had many brothers and sisters. They lived in the White House with many pets. His brothers and sisters took their pets upstairs to cheer up Archie. Soon, his room was full of animals.

He counted two dogs, three cats, a snake, four mice, a rat, and a parrot. "Do you feel better now?" asked Quentin.

Archie frowned. "I still feel sick."

Then Quentin had an idea. He ran downstairs and got another animal. His pet was so big that it had to make a special trip upstairs in the White House elevator.

Archie looked so surprised when Quentin opened his bedroom door. There stood a Shetland pony!

"Now I feel better!" cried Archie.

STORY QUESTIONS

1. Where do Archie and his brothers and sisters live?

a. in a zoo

b. on a farm

c. in an elevator

d. in the White House

2. Why do the kids take their pets upstairs?

a. to make their mother mad

b. to cheer up their sick brother

c. to ride horses

d. to be naughty

3. How does the pony get upstairs?

a. He takes the escalator.

b. He climbs the stairs.

c. He rides the elevator.

d. He comes in through the window.

4. What can you say about the Roosevelt kids?

a. They don't like each other.

b. They are afraid of animals.

c. They don't like Archie.

d. They love their pets.

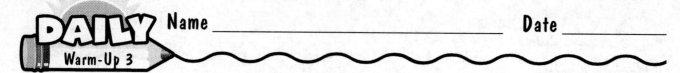

Name _____ **Date** _____

THE LADY WITH A LAMP

Florence Nightingale wanted to be a nurse. Friends laughed at her. "It's a dirty job," they said. "You'll hate it."

Florence didn't care what they said. She read books, and she went to visit hospitals. She became a nurse. But her friends were right about one thing. It was a dirty job.

One day, she walked into a building to find soldiers on bare beds. Even though they were hurt, they didn't have a pillow or blanket. Rats ran around them. Bugs bit them. Dirt was everywhere.

"I will help these men," Florence said. She cleaned each room. She chased away the bugs and rats. She worked twenty hours a day to nurse the men back to health. At night, she held up a lantern to make sure each man's room was clean. That is why they loved her. They called her "The Lady with a Lamp."

STORY QUESTIONS

1. Florence is called "The Lady with a Lamp," because
   a. she has nice furniture.
   b. she is a nurse.
   c. she holds up a lantern to check each man's room.
   d. she has a dirty job.

2. What do Florence's friends say about being a nurse?
   a. Men will love you.   c. There are rats and bugs.
   b. It is a dirty job.   d. You will love this job.

3. What does Florence do when she sees the soldiers?
   a. She runs away.   c. She finds a lamp.
   b. She yells at them.   d. She cleans their rooms.

4. What can you say about Florence?
   a. She is kind and loving.   c. She is lazy.
   b. She is dirty and mean.   d. She is afraid of dirt.

                                       ©Teacher Created Resources, Inc.

DAILY Warm-Up 4

Name _____   Date _____

THE RED FLOWER

Billy didn't like to dress up. He yelled when he had to put on his nice pants. He didn't want to wear a good coat. He didn't like shoes. "I want to run and play outside," he said. "I want to roll in the flowers and climb trees."

"Someday, you will be a man," his father said. "Then, you will have to dress up."

"Never!" said Billy.

But Billy grew up to be William McKinley, president of the United States. Now, he had to dress up. Every morning, he pulled on pants with stripes on them. He put on a stiff white shirt and a coat. He had to wear a tie and a hat!

Still, Billy never forgot his love for flowers. Every day that he was president, he wore a red flower in his buttonhole. That way, he could remember being a boy.

STORY QUESTIONS

1. As a boy, Billy liked . . .
- a. nice clothes.
- b. being president.
- c. top hats.
- d. playing outside.

2. Billy's father says he will have to dress up when he . . .
- a. goes to school.
- b. becomes a man.
- c. wears a flower.
- d. climbs trees.

3. Billy grows up to become . . .
- a. a boy.
- b. William McKinley.
- c. his father.
- d. messy.

4. Why does Billy wear a red flower?
- a. to remember being a boy
- b. because he loves to dress up
- c. because his father tells him to
- d. because he doesn't like yellow flowers

DAILY
Warm-Up 5

Name _____   Date _____

I DARE YOU

Madge loved mystery books. She read them all day long. Her favorite mystery book was Sherlock Holmes.

"All you do is read," cried her little sister Agatha. "You never play with me."

Madge gave Agatha a book. "Read this," she said. "It is a mystery story about Sherlock Holmes. You will love it."

She was right. Agatha did love the book, but she pretended that she did not. "Anyone can write a mystery," she said. "It is no big deal."

Madge smiled. "Really? I dare you to write one yourself!"

Agatha took the dare. She wrote a mystery book. She went on to write 68 more, plus 100 short stories. Agatha Christie became a much-loved writer because of a dare.

STORY QUESTIONS

1. Agatha is sad because Madge . . .
   a. won't play with her.
   b. hates mystery books.
   c. writes mystery books.
   d. dares her to write.

2. What does Agatha say about mystery books?
   a. They are silly.
   b. They are boring.
   c. Anyone can write one.
   d. No one can write one.

3. Why does Agatha write a mystery book?
   a. Her sister makes her write one.
   b. She thinks they are bad.
   c. Her sister dares her to write one.
   d. Her sister writes one.

4. Agatha's last name is . . .
   a. Madge.
   b. Christie.
   c. Mystery.
   d. Holmes.

108

DAILY Warm-Up 6   Name _____ Date _____

THE GOOD MOTHER

Mother Teresa lived in India. She taught high school. One day, she walked into the city. She saw sick people lying in the road. "Help me!" cried a thin man. "I must have water."

"I have to help these people," said Mother Teresa.

She left her school. She found a group of women. They all said they would help poor people, too. The woman gave the poor children food. They took care of the sick mothers and fathers.

One day, she met a happy man. "You gave me water," he said. "You saved my life."

Mother Teresa had only a few clothes. She did not have much money. But she felt very rich. She gave hope to many people. They loved her because she was so good.

STORY QUESTIONS

1. Mother Teresa lived in . . .
   a. a school.   c. India.
   b. the street.   d. America.

2. Why does Mother Teresa want to help people?
   a. because they are students   c. because they have water
   b. because they are poor   d. because they are rich

3. Mother Teresa felt rich because . . .
   a. she had money.   c. she taught school.
   b. she had many clothes.   d. many people loved her.

4. In this story, Mother Teresa is . . .
   a. good.
   b. sad.
   c. tired.
   d. sick.

DAILY Warm-Up 7

Name _____

Date _____

THE BATHTUB

Bill Taft loved to eat. At breakfast, he ate three bowls of oatmeal. At lunch, he ate four peanut butter sandwiches. He ate six apples for snack, and nine cookies. Dinner was the biggest meal of all. Then, Bill ate five pork chops, ten baked potatoes, and a whole apple pie!

Bill Taft became president. He was happy, but he had a problem. He was too fat to fit into the bathtub in the White House. "How will I take a bath?" he asked.

"Maybe you should not eat so much," his wife said.

"But I love to eat!" he cried. "And I have to be clean."

His staff thought and thought. Finally, they said, "We will have to build a special bathtub for you."

They built the biggest bathtub in the world. Four men could fit into it at once—four small men, of course. When Bill got into the tub, he smiled. "Perfect!" he said.

STORY QUESTIONS

1. The biggest meal of Bill's day is . . .
    a. breakfast.
    b. dinner.
    c. lunch.
    d. snack.

2. Why can't Bill fit into the White House bathtub?
    a. He is too fat.
    b. He is too tall.
    c. He is too short.
    d. He is too clean.

3. From this story, you can guess that Bill is as big as . . .
    a. his wife.
    b. four men.
    c. a president.
    d. the White House.

4. Bill is happy because . . .
    a. he doesn't like to be clean.
    b. he can fit into his special bathtub.
    c. he doesn't like to eat.
    d. he is dirty.

Name _____ **Date** _____

ROSA ON THE BUS

Rosa Parks was tired. She had been sewing all day. She got on the bus and sat down, but the bus driver told her to move.

"No," said Rosa. "I need to sit down."

The bus driver was mad. Rosa was black. He said it was a rule that she should stand so that white people could sit down.

"No," said Rosa again.

She was brave. Because of her, people stopped riding the bus. They said that black people should get to sit down, just like white people. They would not ride the bus again until the problem was solved.

Rosa went to court in Alabama, and she won. Now, all people could sit down on the bus. Thank you, Rosa!

STORY QUESTIONS

1. Why does Rosa want to sit down?

   a. She is black.   c. She is mean.

   b. She is white.   d. She is tired.

2. The bus driver said Rosa should stand because . . .

   a. she is a woman.   c. she is black.

   b. she is white.   d. she can sew.

3. In this story, Rosa is . . .

   a. silly.   c. scared.

   b. brave.   d. white.

4. People stopped riding the bus because . . .

   a. rules were not fair.

   b. it cost too much.

   c. Rosa was on it.

   d. they were tired.

DAILY
Warm-Up 9

Name _____

Date _____

FRANKLIN'S PROBLEM

Franklin Roosevelt was our president, but he felt bad. He knew that some people did not have food. Other people did not have a place to live. Old people did not have money.

"What can I do?" thought Franklin. "How can I help all these people?"

He worked to make new jobs. He gave people roads to build and murals to paint. That way, they could buy food. They could also find a place to live. He set aside money for old people to use when they could not work any more.

Franklin Roosevelt helped many people while he was president. They called his work "The New Deal." They loved him for it.

STORY QUESTIONS

1. Why does Franklin feel bad?
  a. because he has no money
  b. because people do not have food
  c. because he lives in the White House
  d. because he is a president

2. Franklin gives people . . .
  a. a home in the White House.   c. old people.
  b. jobs.   d. apples.

3. In this story, one new job was . . .
  a. building roads.   c. building the White House.
  b. painting roads.   d. painting the White House.

4. Franklin's work is called . . .
  a. "The Old Deal."   c. "The New Work."
  b. "Food and Money."   d. "The New Deal."

DAILY
Warm-Up 10

Name _____ **Date** _____

ANNE'S DIARY

Anne Frank liked to write in her diary. When she was 13, her family had to run away from their home. There was a war. People wanted to <u>hurt</u> them. They had to hide. They did not have much food to eat. They felt crowded into a few rooms.

"Why do you write so much?" cried her sister. "Why not help Mother cook and clean?"

"I love to write," Anne replied. She wrote about how she was scared. But she also wrote about the good times she had with her family. She was a brave girl and a good writer.

Now, Anne's diary helps us to know what her life was like during a war. When we read it, we feel sad. We feel mad at people who wanted to hurt her and her sister. But we also feel brave and full of hope, just like Anne.

STORY QUESTIONS

1. Why does Anne's family have to hide?
   a. People want to hurt them.
   b. They don't like her diary.
   c. They don't like their house.
   d. Anne is a bad writer.

2. In this story, Anne is . . .
   a. a coward.   c. in her house.
   b. full of hope.   d. not a writer.

3. Anne wrote her diary during . . .
   a. a storm.   c. a war.
   b. school.   d. dinner.

4. In this story, *hurt* means . . .
   a. sad.   c. cry.
   b. injure.   d. pinch.

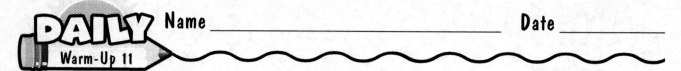

Name _____ **Date** _____

Warm-Up 11

THE GIRL PAINTER

Mary Cassatt wanted to be a painter. Her family was rich. They lived in Paris for a while. There, Mary saw all sorts of art. Then they returned to America.

"I want to be an artist," she told her parents. "I want to paint pictures."

"Nonsense," said her father. "You are a girl."

"Get married. Have children of your own," said her mother.

But Mary begged and begged. At last, her parents let her go to art school. There, she learned to paint pictures. She moved back to Paris.

Men were mad. "A girl painter?" they cried. Then they saw her art. Mary had become a great painter. Thanks to her, both men and women can work as artists.

STORY QUESTIONS

1. In Paris, Mary saw all sorts of . . .
   a. men.
   b. children.
   c. money.
   d. art.

2. Mary's father thought that . . .
   a. she was smart.
   b. she was a boy.
   c. she was an artist.
   d. girls could not be artists.

3. What did Mary learn in art school?
   a. how to make money
   b. how to go to Paris
   c. how to paint pictures
   d. how to use a camera

4. Men in Paris saw that . . .
   a. Mary was a bad painter.
   b. Mary had become a great painter.
   c. Mary was rich.
   d. Mary could not be an artist.

DAILY **Name** _____ **Date** _____

Warm-Up 12

MOZART AND MUSIC

Once, there was a boy named Mozart. When he was three years old, Father taught him to play the organ. "My son makes amazing music," Father said.

"You are wrong," said the king. "He is only three years old. He is a little boy."

"He can play with a blindfold over his eyes," said Father.

"I do not believe you," said the King. "Bring the boy here and prove this to me."

So Father dressed Mozart in a little jacket. He took him to the King. Mozart sat in front of the organ. He let Father put a blindfold around his eyes.

Mozart began to play the organ. The King's eyes got big and round. "I am sorry," he said. "You are right. Mozart makes amazing music!"

STORY QUESTIONS

1. Mozart learns to play the organ when he is . . .

   a. a man.   c. three years old.

   b. a father.   d. thirty years old.

2. Father says Mozart can play the organ without . . .

   a. seeing.   c. touching.

   b. hearing.   d. tasting.

3. Who is wrong in this story?

   a. Mozart   c. the organ

   b. the King   d. Father

4. The King says that Mozart's music is . . .

   a. wrong.

   b. ugly.

   c. loud.

   d. amazing.

DAILY
Warm-Up 13

Name _____

Date _____

SMOKEY THE BEAR

"There is a big fire in New Mexico!" The call came at Station Nine. Mark heard it. He jumped into the fire truck and raced to the forest.

Trees were on fire. Mark and the other firefighters threw water on the flames. Something cried out, and Mark looked up. There in a tree was a bear cub.

"We have to <u>save</u> him!" Mark cried. He moved a ladder to the tree and climbed up. He took the bear cub and wrapped it in his coat. "You are safe now," Mark said.

The cub went to live at the zoo in Washington, D.C. He was called Smokey the Bear. An artist drew him as a cartoon. It reminded people never to play with fire.

STORY QUESTIONS

1. What is Mark's job?
a. He works at a zoo.
b. He is a bear trainer.
c. He is a firefighter.
d. He is a race car driver.

2. Where does Mark find Smokey?
a. in a tree
b. at the zoo
c. in his truck
d. in his coat

3. In this story, *save* means . . .
a. piggy bank.
b. money.
c. hurt.
d. rescue.

4. The cartoon of Smokey reminds people . . .
a. to catch bears.
b. to draw cartoons.
c. to light fires.
d. to never play with fire.

116

©Teacher Created Resources, Inc.

DAILY
Warm-Up 14

Name _____ Date _____

PAT'S MUSIC

Pat Gilmore loved music. His father took him to a meeting in Ireland. There, Pat heard his first band. "I want to make music, too," he said. He learned to play the trumpet.

At 19 years old, Pat talked to his brother. "Let us go to America," he said. "I want to play my trumpet in Boston." He and his brother took a ship across the sea.

In Boston, Pat led two bands. Then, Abraham Lincoln wrote to him. "The war is over," Abe said. "Let us have a party with music."

Then, Pat got together a big band. He asked 5,000 kids to sing. There was even a cannon at the party! Pat was happy. He played his trumpet. A little boy heard him and said to his father, "I want to make music, too."

STORY QUESTIONS

1. Where does Pat hear his first band?

   a. in Boston   c. on a ship

   b. at a party   d. at a meeting

2. Where does Pat want to play his trumpet?

   a. in Ireland   c. in a war

   b. in Boston   d. in a cannon

3. Why does Abraham Lincoln want a party?

   a. because the war is over

   b. because he loves music

   c. because he plays the trumpet

   d. because he likes the cannon

4. Who hears Pat play the trumpet?

   a. his father   c. a dog

   b. a little boy   d. beauty

DAILY
Warm-Up 15

Name _____

Date _____

KAT'S POEM

Katharine Bates looked out the window of the train. There was the tallest mountain she had ever seen. "Pike's Peak," she said. "Amazing."

Kat loved to write. She wrote books about travel, books for kids, and short stories. When she got back to her home, she wrote a poem about the mountain. This poem would make her famous.

"Look at Kat's poem in the newspaper!" a man said to his friend.

"It is beautiful!" the friend said.

People liked Kat's poem so much that they put it to music. "For purple mountain's <u>majesty</u>," they sang.

Kat's poem became the song called "America the Beautiful." We still sing her words today. When you sing them, remember Kat!

STORY QUESTIONS

1. On the train, Kat sees . . .
   a. a newspaper.   c. a mountain.
   b. a poem.   d. a cat.

2. Kat writes . . .
   a. books and poems.   c. only books.
   b. only poems.   d. books, poems, and movies.

3. Why do people sing Kat's poem?
   a. They love the words.
   b. They love to write.
   c. They do not like poems.
   d. They can not play the piano.

4. In this story, *majesty* means . . .
   a. a king.   c. Kat.
   b. a queen.   d. beauty.

 ©Teacher Created Resources, Inc.

DAILY Warm-Up 16   Name _____   Date _____

THE LIBERTY BELL

Tom had a problem. The men in the United States asked him to make a liberty bell to show that they were free. He worked hard on the bell. He sent it on a boat from England to the United States. But when the men rang it, the bell cracked!

"Try again!" the men said. So Tom melted down the bell. He used the metal in it to make another one.

"This time it will not crack," he said. But when the men rang it, the bell cracked again.

"Try again!" the men said. Tom made a third bell. The men rang it. It did not crack.

People rang that bell on the Fourth of July for eighty-one years. On the eighty-second year, they rang the bell again, and what do you think happened? It cracked!

STORY QUESTIONS

1. What is Tom's problem?
   a. He doesn't like the United States.
   b. He is not free.
   c. His bell is perfect.
   d. The liberty bell keeps cracking.

2. What does Tom do with the first bell?
   a. He throws it away.   c. He rings it.
   b. He kicks it.   d. He melts it down.

3. What happens to Tom's second bell?
   a. It rings for eighty-one years.   c. It falls on Tom.
   b. It works well.   d. It cracks.

4. The liberty bell is a symbol of . . .
   a. freedom.   c. metal.
   b. cracks.   d. England.

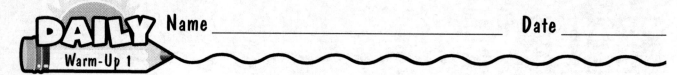

Name _____ **Date** _____

STUART'S STUFF

Stuart loved to take things that didn't belong to him. He took his father's razor. He took his mother's book. He put them in a box under his bed to look at.

"Where is my razor?" cried Father. "I can't shave!"

"Where is my book?" cried Mother. "I need to study!"

Stuart stayed silent. He closed his door and opened the box to look at his stuff.

Then one day, he couldn't find his baseball glove. His basketball and racecar were missing, too. He felt very sad. He told his father someone had stolen his toys.

There on his father's desk were the glove, the ball, and the car. "Don't take things that don't belong to you," Father said. Right away, Stuart returned his father's razor. He returned his mother's book. He promised never to take their things again.

STORY QUESTIONS

1. Why does Stuart like to take things?
    a. He likes to sell them.
    b. He likes to look at them.
    c. He likes to make people mad.
    d. He likes to use them.

2. Why can't Mother study?
    a. Her roller blades are gone.
    b. Her razor is gone.
    c. She is too busy.
    d. Her book is gone.

3. Why does Stuart's father take his toys?
    a. to teach him a lesson
    b. to play with them
    c. to look at them
    d. to help Mother study

4. In this story, Stuart learns . . .
    a. to steal.
    b. to roller blade.
    c. to shave.
    d. to leave other people's items alone.

DAILY Warm-Up 2 Name _____ Date _____

THE SMALL GIRL

Sarah Small was the smallest girl in second grade. She could not reach the water fountain. She felt very sad.

"Wait and see," said Mother. "It's good to be small."

One day, Sarah and her friends were playing soccer. Sarah was good at soccer. She was so small that she could run through tall people's legs. She had just kicked the ball when she saw something green and white.

There was a five-dollar bill on the other side of the fence, beside a small hole. Sarah's friends were too big to fit through the hole to reach it. But Sarah got down on her hands and knees and slipped through. She picked up the bill from off the ground. Then she told her friends she would buy them all ice cream. "Sometimes, it's good to be small!" she said.

STORY QUESTIONS

1. Why is Sarah sad?
   a. because she finds five dollars
   b. because she buys ice cream
   c. because she plays soccer
   d. because she is small

2. Why is Sarah good at soccer?
   a. because she can run through legs
   b. because she finds five dollars
   c. because she is tough
   d. because she can crawl through holes

3. What does Sarah find on the ground?
   a. a soccer ball
   b. a five-dollar bill
   c. ice cream
   d. a worm

4. What does Sarah do with the money?
   a. She shares it.
   b. She hides it.
   c. She leaves it there.
   d. She buys ice cream for herself.

DAILY
Warm-Up 3

Name _____   Date _____

MARK

Mark was seven years old. He talked slowly. He could not read yet. But he was a fast runner.

Mark did not have friends at school. The other kids stayed away from him because he looked different. His head was big. His arms and legs were short. People were afraid.

One day, it was time to run relay races. No one picked Mark to be on his or her team. "Run on Scott's team," the teacher said. Scott made an angry face.

Mark ran last. Scott's team was behind. But Mark ran and ran. He ran so fast that he caught up to the front runner. Thanks to Mark, Scott's team won the relay.

"Hurrah!" all the kids cried. They picked Mark up in the air and cheered for him. Now they weren't scared. They all wanted Mark to run on their team.

STORY QUESTIONS

1. Why are kids afraid of Mark?
   a. He looks different.
   b. He can run fast.
   c. He hits people.
   d. He talks too fast.

2. Mark is really good at . . .
   a. reading.
   b. being scared.
   c. running.
   d. talking.

3. Why is Scott happy?
   a. Mark wins the relay.
   b. Mark is not on his team.
   c. His team loses the relay.
   d. The kids pick up Scott.

4. The message in this story is . . .
   a. you should be scared of people.
   b. watch out for people who can't read.
   c. everyone has a talent.
   d. some people can't do anything well.

Name _____ Date _____

TAMALES

Mondo's mother made tamales at Christmas. They were made with chicken or beef. "Tamales remind me of Christmas," Mondo said.

His friends laughed. "Tamales aren't Christmas food," they said. "We eat gingerbread men and candy canes."

Mondo felt sad. He went to his mother. "Why don't we bake gingerbread men for Christmas?" he asked.

She smiled. "Our tamales are special," she said. "My mother made them for me when I was a child. Her mother made them for her. Ask your friends over to try them."

Mondo asked his friends to come over. They began to eat the tamales. Then, something amazing happened. They ate and they ate. They even asked for more! "We wish our mothers would make tamales for Christmas," they said to Mondo. He just smiled and ate another tamale.

STORY QUESTIONS

1. What reminds Mondo of Christmas?
   a. chicken
   b. gingerbread men
   c. tamales
   d. candy canes

2. Mondo's friends think Christmas food is . . .
   a. tamales.
   b. beef.
   c. chicken.
   d. gingerbread.

3. What happens when Mondo's friends try the tamales?
   a. They ask for more.
   b. They spit them out.
   c. They laugh at him.
   d. They don't like the tamales.

4. Why does Mondo's mother make tamales for Christmas?
   a. because they are easy
   b. because her mother made them for her
   c. because they have chicken
   d. because they make her sad

DAILY
Warm-Up 5

Name _____ Date _____

THE DOG

Molly wanted a dog more than anything. Every night, she asked Mom, "Please, may we get a dog?" Every morning, she said to Dad, "A dog would be a good thing to have."

"Dogs are work," said Mom. "You have to walk them every day."

"You have to feed them and brush them," said Dad. "They need <u>fresh</u> water, too."

"I will take good care of a dog," Molly said. "I will walk him and feed him. I will brush him and make sure he always has clean water."

Her parents said nothing. Molly felt sad. "I will never get a dog," she said.

On her seventh birthday, a box sat on the floor. "For Molly," said the tag. The box wiggled. Then it barked. "My dog!" cried Molly.

STORY QUESTIONS

1. Every day, dogs need . . .
   a. a box.
   b. a walk.
   c. a birthday.
   d. a little girl.

2. In this story, *fresh* means . . .
   a. air.
   b. lettuce.
   c. clean.
   d. bright.

3. Where does Molly find the puppy?
   a. on a leash
   b. at the store
   c. in a box
   d. outside

4. Why do Molly's parents get her a dog?
   a. because she will take care of it
   b. because she cries
   c. because she can walk
   d. because they will take care of it

THE FIREFIGHTER

Julie wanted to be a firefighter when she grew up. "I will put out fires," she told her friends at lunch. "I will save people. I will even drive a fire truck."

The boys in her class laughed. "Only men can be firefighters," they said. "Women are not strong. They cannot lift a heavy hose or carry people to safety. Women are too short to drive a fire truck."

"Women can be firefighters," Julie said. "You'll see."

The next day was Show and Tell. Julie went first. "I would like you to meet someone," she told her class. Just then, a tall, strong woman walked in. She wore yellow firefighter's clothes and a tall yellow hat. She carried a heavy hose. Julie smiled. "This is my sister, Jean. She is a firefighter."

STORY QUESTIONS

1. Julie's sister is . . .

   a. not very strong.

   b. short.

   c. yellow.

   d. a firefighter.

2. Firefighters must be . . .

   a. men.

   b. strong.

   c. boys.

   d. mean.

3. Why do the boys laugh at Julie?

   a. because she is silly

   b. because she is wrong

   c. because they think only men can be firefighters

   d. because of her sister

4. What does Julie show the class?

   a. Both men and women can be firefighters.

   b. Firefighters wear strange clothes.

   c. Watch out for the heavy hose.

   d. Her sister is wrong.

DAILY Warm-Up 7   Name _____   Date _____

GRANDMA IS SICK

Grandma baked Jim cookies. She sewed his clothes. She even fixed his bike tire when it was flat.

But one day, Grandma felt sick. "I am too tired to bake cookies and fix bikes," she told Jim. "I don't even feel well enough to sew."

Grandma was sick for weeks and weeks. Jim felt very sad. "Grandma can't take care of me," he told his father.

Dad thought about this. "Maybe you can take care of her."

Dad helped Jim to bake Grandma's favorite carrot cake. He helped Jim to make a *Get Well* card. He even helped Jim to fix the flat tire on Grandma's bike. "That way, when she feels better, she can ride," Dad said.

Grandma took a bite of cake. She looked at the card and at her bike. Then she gave Jim a big hug. "Thank you for taking care of me," she said. "I feel better already!"

STORY QUESTIONS

1. What does Grandma do for Jim?
   a. She bakes carrot cake.
   b. She sews his clothes.
   c. She makes "Get Well" cards.
   d. She gets sick.

2. Why is Jim sad?
   a. because he is sick
   b. because his bike has a flat tire
   c. because Dad is mad at him
   d. because Grandma is sick

3. What does Jim do for Grandma?
   a. He fixes her bike.
   b. He makes her cookies.
   c. He sews a shirt.
   d. He makes a birthday card.

4. Grandma is thankful because . . .
   a. Jim takes care of her.
   b. She can ride a bike.
   c. She doesn't like cake.
   d. She is sick.

THE BEAN PLANT

Sue loved plants. She wanted a garden. But she lived in an apartment with no backyard. "I wish I had a garden," she said.

One day, her mother gave her a bean seed. It was small and white. "Plant this seed in a paper cup," Mom said. "Put the cup beside your window. Water the dirt when it looks dry. Then, wait and see."

Sue put dirt in a paper cup. She planted the bean seed in the dirt and put the cup next to the window. Whenever the dirt looked dry, she gave it water. Nothing happened.

Then one day, a little green sprout stuck up, with two green leaves. "It's a bean plant!" Sue cried. She made sure the plant got sunlight and water. It got bigger, and she had to put it in a pot. In three months, it grew into a big, strong plant. Green beans hung on it. Sue picked the beans, and her parents cooked them for dinner.

STORY QUESTIONS

1. Why can't Sue have a garden?
   a. She doesn't like plants.
   b. She doesn't have a backyard.
   c. She doesn't like gardens.
   d. Her parents are mean.

2. What does Mom give Sue?
   a. a paper cup
   b. a tomato seed

   c. a backyard
   d. a bean seed

3. What does Sue give to the bean seed?
   a. water and sunlight
   b. water and green beans

   c. green beans and sunlight
   d. a backyard

4. Why does Sue put her plant into a pot?
   a. because it is small
   b. because it grows bigger

   c. because it is green
   d. so she can eat it

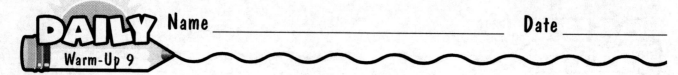

DAILY Warm-Up 9

Name _____

Date _____

THE STRAY CAT

One day, Ann walked home from school. A cat began to follow her. He had long black fur. He did not wear a collar or a nametag. She picked him up, and he purred.

"Please, may I keep this cat?" Ann asked her parents.

"What if he belongs to someone?" they said.

Mom called the animal shelter to find out if anyone had lost a black cat. Dad put up "Found Cat" signs and took the cat to the vet for a checkup. Ann carried the cat from door to door. "Do you know this cat?" she asked.

"No," said everyone. "We don't know who he belongs to." No one at the shelter had lost a black cat. No one called about the "Found Cat" signs. Ann took care of the cat for two weeks. She fed the cat and gave him water. Finally, her parents said the magic words: "The cat is yours, Ann!"

STORY QUESTIONS

1. The cat does not have . . .
- a. long black fur.
- b. a nametag.
- c. a vet.
- d. a purr.

2. Ann's parents try to find the cat's owner by . . .
- a. calling the owner.
- b. going door to door.
- c. saying the magic words.
- d. putting up signs and calling the animal shelter.

3. How long does Ann wait to find the cat's owner?
- a. two weeks
- b. two days
- c. two months
- d. forever

4. Why do Ann's parents give her the cat?
- a. because he is black
- b. because he purrs
- c. because they can't find his owner
- d. because they are magic

DAILY Name _____ Date _____

Warm-Up 10

NEW BABY

Roni was sad. Lately, Mother was always tired. She didn't want to <u>play</u> hide and seek or bake cookies. She just wanted to sleep on the couch.

"What is wrong with Mother?" Roni asked Father. "She doesn't want to play with me any more."

He smiled. "Mother is resting," he said. "Soon, you will have a baby brother."

Then Mother went into the hospital. Father took Roni to visit her that night. She held a little baby in a blanket.

Roni looked at the little baby. She frowned. "Will you ever want to play hide and seek again?"

"Yes," Mother said. "Soon, this little boy will be able to play, too." Then Roni wasn't sad anymore. She knew now that having a brother would be fun.

STORY QUESTIONS

1. Why is Mother tired?
   a. because she bakes cookies
   b. because she is in the hospital
   c. because she is going to have a baby
   d. because she is sad

2. In this story, Father is . . .
   a. sad.   c. tired.
   b. mad.   d. happy.

3. Roni knows that having a brother will be . . .
   a. tiring.   c. scary.
   b. fun.   d. sad.

4. In this story, *play* means . . .
   a. have fun.   c. perform.
   b. theater.   d. piano.

DAILY Warm-Up 11

Name _____

Date _____

THE AIRPLANE

Bill wanted to see his grandparents, but there was a problem. They lived in New York. He lived in Oregon. Bill was afraid to fly in an airplane.

"It's fun," said George. "It's like being a bird."

"You can have whatever you want to drink on an airplane," said Lola. "Even soda!"

"It's too high," Bill said. "I like to be on the ground."

Then one day, Grandpa invited Bill for his birthday. "I will pay for your plane ticket," he said.

Bill tried to be brave. He walked behind his parents up to the plane. He sat down in his seat. Then, the plane took off. Bill's hands were wet with sweat. But outside, he saw fluffy white clouds. They were pretty! A woman brought him ginger ale. Flying wasn't so scary after all!

STORY QUESTIONS

1. Why doesn't Bill want to fly?
   a. He says it's too high up.
   b. He says he doesn't like soda.
   c. He says he doesn't like birds.
   d. He says flying is fun.

2. Why does Bill decide to fly?
   a. because Grandpa invites him to New York
   b. because he loves to fly
   c. because Grandpa invites him to Oregon
   d. because he is a bird

3. On the plane, Bill's hands are wet with . . .
   a. sweat.
   b. soda.
   c. rain.
   d. ginger ale.

4. What does Bill find out about the clouds?
   a. They are black.
   b. They are ugly.
   c. They are too high up.
   d. They are pretty.

DAILY Name _____ Date _____
Warm-Up 12

THE COMPUTER

Everyone at Jonah's school had a computer. They knew how to play games on it. They knew how to type. They even knew how to listen to music on their computer.

"We can't afford a new computer right now," said Dad.

But Jonah came up with a plan. "Dad didn't say anything about an old computer," he thought.

Jonah mowed the lawn for Mrs. Sanchez. He walked Mr. Frank's dog. He weeded the Smiths' flower bed. He saved money in his piggy bank.

Finally, he asked Dad to drive to the used computer store. "The owner takes people's old computers and cleans them up," Jonah said. "Then he sells them for a little money."

"But how will we pay for it?" Dad asked.

Jonah shook his piggy bank full of quarters and dimes and nickels. "I worked hard and saved money," he said proudly.

STORY QUESTIONS

1. Why can't Jonah get a new computer?
   a. His family can't afford one.
   b. Everyone else has one.
   c. He doesn't work hard.
   d. He sold his old computer.

2. In this story, Jonah is . . .
   a. lazy.
   b. sad.
   c. hard-working.
   d. angry.

3. Why does Jonah want to buy an old computer?
   a. because it is better
   b. because it plays games
   c. because it is clean
   d. because it doesn't cost as much

4. In this story, Jonah is proud because . . .
   a. he walks dogs.
   b. he works hard and saves money.
   c. he doesn't have a computer.
   d. he weeds the flower bed.

DAILY Warm-Up 13

Name _____

Date _____

SPIDERS

Holly was afraid of spiders. She thought their eight legs were creepy. She cried whenever she saw one.

Holly had a brother named Fred. Fred loved to tease Holly. He would put a spider in a jar under her pillow. He hung a plastic spider from her chair. Holly cried and cried.

One day, Mama said, "Without spiders, we would have too many flies. If you like them, Fred will stop teasing you."

Holly looked at a garden spider on a web. It looked back at her. Would it jump on her? But the spider just sat there.

Holly realized that the spider was pretty. It caught a fly in its web. "Amazing," thought Holly.

The next time Fred teased her with a plastic spider, she laughed. When she found a jar under her pillow, Holly let the spider go outside. "Catch a lot of flies," she said.

STORY QUESTIONS

1. Why is Holly afraid of spiders?
   a. She knows they catch flies.
   b. They are plastic.
   c. They have creepy legs.
   d. Her brother likes them.

2. What does Fred like to hang on Holly's chair?
   a. a plastic spider
   b. a spider in a jar
   c. a spider web
   d. a fly

3. What does Holly find out about spiders?
   a. They are plastic.
   b. They are scary.
   c. They are mean.
   d. They are amazing.

4. Fred will probably stop teasing Holly because . . .
   a. she just laughs.
   b. she cries.
   c. she doesn't like spiders.
   d. she is afraid of him.

DAILY
Warm-Up 14

Name _____ Date _____

THE LIE

Lisa always told the truth. "I will not tell a lie," she said. But one day, she didn't know what to do.

She and her friend Jan went shopping with their fathers. Jan found a sweater. "I love it," she cried. "Don't you love it, too, Lisa?"

The sweater was bright yellow. It was fuzzy like a baby duck's <u>down</u>. It had a big orange balloon on the front. Lisa thought it was ugly. She didn't want to hurt Jan.

She looked at the sweater. She thought about what to say. She did not want to tell a lie. Finally, she said, "It is very bright. It looks soft. I'm glad that you love it."

Jan bought the sweater. She wore it a lot. Lisa was a good friend. She never said the sweater was ugly, and she never told a lie.

STORY QUESTIONS

1. Why does Lisa have a problem?
   a. She doesn't love Jan's sweater.
   b. She likes to lie.
   c. She never tells the truth.
   d. She wants Jan's sweater.

2. In this story, *down* means . . .
   a. below.   c. under.
   b. feathers.   d. feet.

3. Lisa tells Jan that the sweater is . . .
   a. ugly.   c. orange.
   b. beautiful.   d. bright.

4. In this story, Lisa is . . .
   a. a liar.   c. honest.
   b. soft.   d. ugly.

Name _____

Date _____

FRANK'S BEDROOM

Frank never cleaned his room. Books and clothes covered his floor. His bed was never made. "Please clean your room," Father said.

Frank kicked his clothes and books under the bed. "All clean," he said.

Frank was old enough to clean his room. But he was lazy. One day, his parents came up with a plan.

"Let's go to the ball game," said Mother. "Don't forget your mitt."

Frank ran to look for his mitt. But his room was so messy. He stuffed his clothes into the dresser—no mitt. He put his books on the shelf—no mitt. He made his bed and looked under it. No mitt!

"Too late," Father said. "We have missed the game."

Frank felt sad. But now his room was clean, except for his closet. He began to clean it. There on the floor was his mitt! "I will keep my room clean from now on," he said.

STORY QUESTIONS

1. Why doesn't Frank clean his room?
   a. because he is neat
   b. because he likes baseball
   c. because he is lazy
   d. because he wants dinner

2. In this story, Frank is . . .
   a. old enough to clean his room.
   b. too busy.
   c. five years old.
   d. too young to clean his room.

3. Why does Frank miss the ball game?
   a. He can't find his books.
   b. He can't find his clothes.
   c. He doesn't like baseball.
   d. He can't find his mitt.

4. Why does Frank decide to keep his room clean?
   a. so he can eat dinner
   b. so he can go to the ball game
   c. so he can find his things
   d. so he can be messy

Name _____ **Date** _____

GOING CAMPING

Jenny was afraid to go camping. "Come on, Jenny," said her brother, Mike. "It will be fun. We can take our dog."

They pitched a tent beside a lake. Then, something splashed. "What was that noise?" Jenny cried.

"Only a fish," said Mike.

They roasted corn and bread over the fire. Their dog got a piece of bread, too. Then, something hooted.

"What was that noise?" Jenny cried.

"Only an owl," said Mike.

They crawled into their sleeping bags and zipped up the tent. Then, something whined and scratched on the door.

"What was that noise?" Jenny cried.

Now, Mike was scared, too. He turned on his flashlight. Then he began to laugh. "It's our dog!" he said. "We forgot to put him in the tent with us!"

STORY QUESTIONS

1. Why doesn't Jenny like to camp?

   a. She doesn't like corn.   c. She doesn't like the lake.

   b. She is afraid.   d. She doesn't have a tent.

2. What makes the hooting noise?

   a. a dog   c. Mike

   b. a fish   d. an owl

3. What scratches on the tent door?

   a. the owl   c. a bear

   b. the fish   d. a dog

4. Why does the dog whine?

   a. because he is sick

   b. because he wants to sleep in the tent

   c. because he wants to sleep in the lake

   d. because he is roasting bread

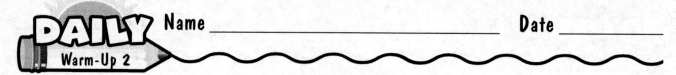

THE NEST

Mother could not find her thread. "I had a whole spool of it," she told the family. "Now it is gone."

Aunt Jean could not find her left black glove. "I can't wear only one glove!" she cried.

Stan hopped up and down in one green sock and one blue sock. "Who would take one green sock?"

Someone had taken Jill's pink hair ribbon. "It's a <u>mystery</u>," she said. "Who is taking our things?"

Stan decided to find out who the thief was. He looked high. He looked low. He opened cabinet doors. Finally, he found the thief.

"It's a mouse!" he said. There in a cabinet was a nest. It was made of shredded newspaper, white thread, a black glove, a green sock, and a pink ribbon. Inside the nest were five mouse babies!

STORY QUESTIONS

1. Who takes Aunt Jean's glove?
   a. Mother
   b. Stan
   c. the cat
   d. a mouse

2. What is Stan missing?
   a. a glove
   b. a blue sock
   c. a green sock
   d. a ribbon

3. In this story, *mystery* means . . .
   a. a novel.
   b. puzzle.
   c. a movie.
   d. mouse.

4. What does Stan find in the cabinet?
   a. a blue sock
   b. three mouse babies
   c. a bird's nest
   d. a pink ribbon

THE KITTEN

"Meow! Meow!" The cries came from a tall tree on Marvin Street.

Kids stopped playing hide and seek. They stopped playing tag. Everyone ran over to the tree. "It's a kitten," Ron said. "We have to save her!"

Ron tried to climb the tree. It was too tall. Susan got a ladder from her house. She tried to reach the kitten. The ladder was too short.

Finally, Joe had an idea. "I'll call the fire department," he said. The fire truck arrived. One man put up a tall ladder. He climbed to the top and rescued the kitten.

"Meow! Meow!" cried the kitten. The firefighter held the kitten. Ron and Susan and Joe got to pet it. Then there was another cry.

"My kitty!" said Mrs. Miller. "Was she on fire?"

STORY QUESTIONS

1. What are the kids playing on Marvin Street?
   a. kick the can
   b. firefighter
   c. hide the cat
   d. tag

2. What does Susan get?
   a. a tall ladder
   b. a short ladder
   c. a fire truck
   d. a kitten

3. Who calls the fire department?
   a. Susan
   b. Joe
   c. Mrs. Miller
   d. Marvin

4. Mrs. Miller thinks her kitten is on fire . . .
   a. because a firefighter is holding it.
   b. because she sees flames.
   c. because the tree is on fire.
   d. because the hose is on.

DAILY Warm-Up 4

Name _____

Date _____

SURFER JIN

Jin liked to surf. "The ocean is powerful," Grandma said. "Don't swim out too far."

But Jin always swam out too far. "The ocean is weak," he said. "It will not hurt me."

One day, Jin swam far out in the water. He sat on his surfboard. He waited for a <u>wave</u>. He didn't see that he was drifting farther and farther out.

Suddenly, the shore looked very small. The ocean was rough. Waves tossed Jin around. He swam and swam toward the shore. He was very tired. A big wave slapped him on the head. He almost lost his surfboard. Finally, he made it to shore.

"You are right," he told Grandma that night. "The ocean is powerful. I will not swim out too far ever again."

STORY QUESTIONS

1. What does Jin learn about the ocean?
   a. It is weak.
   b. It slaps him on the arm.
   c. It is powerful.
   d. It does not have waves.

2. In this story, *wave* means . . .
   a. goodbye.   c. a glass of water.
   b. a crest of water.   d. a hand.

3. Jin almost loses his . . .
   a. surfboard.   c. head.
   b. Grandma.   d. ocean.

4. Why is Jin tired?
   a. He surfs a lot.   c. He has to swim a long way to shore.
   b. He does not sleep.   d. He almost loses his surfboard.

DAILY Name _____ Date _____
Warm-Up 5

THE ADVENTURE

"We are going on an adventure," said Bob to his friends. "We need to be prepared."

Steve brought a rope. "You never know when you will have to pull someone out of quicksand," he said.

Tina brought a whistle. "You never know when you might get lost and have to call someone," she said.

Bob gave them a strange look and put on his backpack. He and his friends climbed over his fence. They jumped over a log. They walked across a brick wall. They waded through a puddle. Finally, they reached a park.

"Where is the quicksand?" Steve twirled his rope.

"I am not lost." Tina put away her whistle.

Bob reached into his backpack. He put down a blanket and pulled out three sandwiches and some cookies. "It's a picnic," he said. "I am prepared. Are you?"

STORY QUESTIONS

1. A different title for this story is . . .
   a. "The Quicksand."   c. "Be Prepared."
   b. "Tina's Whistle."   d. "Bob's Rope."

2. Why does Tina bring a whistle?
   a. in case she sees quicksand   c. to blow in Bob's ears
   b. in case they have a picnic   d. in case they get lost

3. Steve brings a rope to pull someone . . .
   a. out of quicksand.   c. off a brick wall.
   b. out of a puddle.   d. into the picnic.

4. Bob is prepared for . . .
   a. quicksand.
   b. a picnic.
   c. getting lost.
   d. a tornado.

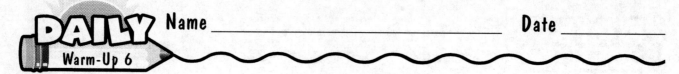

Name _____   **Date** _____

THE NOTE

Dad put spare change in a tin. He put the tin in his sock drawer. Jon found it one day when he was helping to put away clean clothes.

"Wow!" he said to himself. "Dad won't miss a few nickels." He put three nickels in his pocket and went to the store to buy candy.

The next week, he took two dimes. "Dad will never miss them," he said. The week after that, he took three quarters.

The fourth week, Jon sneaked up to Dad's room. He opened the drawer. There in the tin was a note. "Bank robbers start by stealing nickels," said the note.

John felt so bad. He did chores and earned money. Then he put it all back into Dad's tin.

STORY QUESTIONS

1. Dad puts spare change in a . . .
   a. note.
   b. shoe.
   c. sock.
   d. tin.

2. What does Jon buy with three nickels?
   a. socks
   b. candy
   c. a bank robber
   d. clean clothes

3. What does Jon find in the tin?
   a. a note
   b. pennies
   c. a sock
   d. a bank

4. Why does Jon do chores?
   a. so he can rob a bank
   b. so he can buy socks
   c. so he can pay Dad back
   d. so he can buy candy

DAILY Name _____ **Date** _____
Warm-Up 7

THE APPLE THIEF

Mom loved apples. She liked to bake pie. She liked to put them in oatmeal. She liked to eat them right off the tree.

Mom and Maria lived on a farm. They had horses and cows. They had a lot of land. One day, she planted an apple tree. "Now, we can have fresh apples," she told Maria.

First, the tree had flowers. Then it had little green apples. Finally, the apples were red and ripe. "Tomorrow, we will pick them," said Mom.

But the next morning, all the apples were gone. "Did you pick the apples?" Mom asked Maria.

"No," said Maria.

"Then where are they?"

They looked and looked. Then, they saw their black pony. She was <u>lying</u> down. Her tummy was swollen. She looked very full. "Look who ate the apples!" said Mom.

STORY QUESTIONS

1. Why is the pony's tummy swollen?
   a. She has eaten Maria.
   b. She has eaten a tree.
   c. She has eaten flowers.
   d. She has eaten the apples.

2. Where do Mom and Maria live?
   a. in an apple tree
   b. in the horse stall
   c. in a city
   d. on a farm

3. What is **true** about this story?
   a. Mom does not have a horse.
   b. The pony eats all the apples.
   c. Maria eats all the apples.
   d. The pony is white.

4. In this story, *lying* means . . .
   a. resting.
   b. telling a lie.
   c. being dishonest.
   d. sitting on a chair.

DAILY Name _____   Date _____
Warm-Up 8

SCARY STORY

Jill asked her friends to <u>spend</u> the night. They had a slumber party. They told scary stories in the dark.

"Once, there was a goblin," said Jill. "He had a red face and red eyes. He liked to scream in people's ears."

The girls around Jill looked scared. But they wanted to hear the rest of the story. "Keep telling it," they said.

Jill said, "The goblin came to the window one night."

Then Jill looked out the window. There was a red face with red eyes. She screamed. The other girls screamed, too. They were so scared.

Jill turned the light on. Then the girls saw that it wasn't a goblin at all. It was Jill's brother, Travis. He held a flashlight under his chin. It made his face and eyes look red. "You girls scream too loud," Travis said.

STORY QUESTIONS

1. Who does Jill see out the window?
 a. a goblin
 b. a girl
 c. a monster
 d. her brother

2. In this story, *spend* means . . .
 a. stay over.
 b. give money.
 c. buy something.
 d. pay.

3. The girls are telling stories in the . . .
 a. light.
 b. trees.
 c. dark.
 d. daytime.

4. What makes Travis' eyes look red?
 a. a goblin
 b. a flashlight
 c. Jill's story
 d. the scream

DAILY Name _____ **Date** _____

Warm-Up 9

SCHOOL MICE

Missy loved mice. She had two in her room. She gave them food and water every day. When it was time for school, she cried. She didn't want to leave her mice.

One day, the teacher gave a test. The students were very quiet. Everyone was writing. Then, they heard a scratching sound. The teacher looked up. "What is that?" she asked.

But nobody knew. Then, they heard a squeaking sound. "What is that?" asked the teacher. But nobody knew!

The teacher walked around the classroom. She listened for sounds. She heard a rustle. She heard a squeal. The sounds came from Missy's coat. The teacher reached into the pocket. "What is this?" she cried.

There in Missy's coat pocket sat two little mice. "I missed them," said Missy. "They wanted to come to school!"

STORY QUESTIONS

1. Why does Missy cry?
 a. She doesn't like school.
 b. She doesn't like mice.
 c. She doesn't want to leave her mice.
 d. She is sick.

2. What makes the squeaking sound?
 a. Missy
 b. the teacher
 c. the desk
 d. the mice

3. Where does Missy hide her mice?
 a. in her desk
 b. in her coat
 c. in a book
 d. at home

4. Why does Missy bring mice to school?
 a. because she misses them
 b. because they need water
 c. because they take a test
 d. because they are quiet

DAILY Warm-Up 10

Name _____

Date _____

LOST DOG

"Oh no! What will we do?" Brian and Joann had gone hiking in the snow with their dog, Max. Now, Max was gone, and it was almost dark.

"Here, Max! Here, boy!" they called. Brian tried to run. His snowshoes were too big and heavy.

"What if a bear eats our dog?" cried Joann. Just then, she heard a crack and a splash. "Over there!" she yelled.

Brian and Joann ran to the side of a <u>frozen</u> lake. There was Max. He had broken through the ice. Now, he was trying to swim in freezing water.

"Quick, give me your hiking stick," said Brian. "Now, hold onto my leg."

Brian threw himself onto the snow and scooted toward the lake. He held one end of the stick. Joann held the other. Finally, he could reach Max. He grabbed the dog's collar and pulled him out. "You're safe now, boy," he said.

STORY QUESTIONS

1. Where are Brian and Joann hiking?
   a. on a lake
   b. in the sun
   c. in the snow
   d. by a river

2. What happens to Max?
   a. A bear eats him.
   b. He drowns in the lake.
   c. He falls in the lake.
   d. He saves Brian.

3. In this story, *frozen* means . . .
   a. covered with ice.
   b. ice cubes.
   c. ice cream.
   d. blizzard.

4. What is **true** about this story?
   a. Max is wearing a leash.
   b. Joann grabs Max's collar.
   c. Max is wearing a collar.
   d. The lake is not frozen.

DAILY
Warm-Up 11

Name _____ Date _____

DOTS OF FLOUR

Simon was confused. He kept finding dots of flour. They were on the street and under trees, all the way to school.

"Maybe someone had a bag of flour, and it leaked," said his friend Jim.

"Maybe it's not flour at all. Maybe it's space dust from aliens," said his friend Grace.

But they were both wrong. After school, Simon followed the dots of flour to a park. There was a big X made out of flour by a table. "Weird," said Simon to himself.

Just then, a group of people ran up. They wore shorts and T-shirts. "We're playing a game," they said to Simon. "One runner <u>marks</u> a trail with dots of flour. The rest of us run around and try to find the trail. It's a game!"

"It's strange," thought Simon as he walked home. But he was glad he had solved the mystery.

STORY QUESTIONS

1. What does Simon find on the street?
   a. a bag of flour
   b. space dust
   c. a T-shirt
   d. dots of flour

2. Why does Simon follow the flour to the park?
   a. He is a runner.
   b. He wants to solve the mystery.
   c. He wants to go into space.
   d. He is playing a game.

3. In this story, *marks* means . . .
   a. shows.
   b. boys.
   c. runners.
   d. grade.

4. The dots of flour are part of a . . .
   a. school.
   b. cake.
   c. game.
   d. picnic.

DAILY Warm-Up 12

Name _____

Date _____

THE GREEN EYES

Brynnli turned off her light. She was about to get into bed when she saw something. Two green eyes glowed from under the bed.

"Help! Help!" she cried.

Mother ran in. "What is wrong?"

"There is a monster under my bed. It has green eyes."

"Monsters are not real," said Mother. "Go to sleep."

Brynnli tried to sleep. Then, she leaned down over her bed. The green eyes winked. Something hissed.

"Help! Help!" she cried.

Again, Mother ran in. "What is wrong?"

"There is a monster. It has green eyes. It hisses!"

Just then, the phone rang. Mother answered it. It was Mrs. Montez. "Have you seen my cat?" she said.

STORY QUESTIONS

1. Who is under Brynnli's bed?
a. Brynnli
b. a cat
c. Mrs. Montez
d. Mother

2. Mother says that monsters . . .
a. have green eyes.
b. are real.
c. hiss.
d. are not real.

3. What is **true** about this story?
a. Mrs. Montez loses her cat.
b. There is a monster under the bed.
c. Mother winks and hisses.
d. Brynnli sees two blue eyes.

4. What would be another good title for this story?
a. "Dog Monster"
b. "Cat Monster"
c. "The Cat with Yellow Eyes"
d. "The Hissing Snake"

146 ©Teacher Created Resources, Inc.

DAILY Name _____ **Date** _____

Warm-Up 13

THE JUNGLE

Carlos and Maya walked through the old <u>ruins</u> of a city in Mexico. They saw iguanas on the stone walls. They touched rocks that people had used for cooking pots.

"Do not wander into the jungle," said the tour guide. "It is dark and full of danger."

Carlos did not listen. He saw a bright orange bird in a palm tree. It flew away. He followed it into the jungle. Then, he was lost. One tree looked just like another. He could not find the trail. "What will I do?" Carlos cried.

"Sew up the hole in your backpack." Maya walked up to him. "Your sunflower seeds fell out. They made a trail so I could find you. Now, let's get back to our tour guide, fast. Wild animals love sunflower seeds!"

STORY QUESTIONS

1. In this story, *ruins* mean . . .
   a. an old city.
   b. wrecks.
   c. destroys.
   d. hurts.

2. The tour guide says the jungle is . . .
   a. fun.
   b. bright.
   c. dangerous.
   d. old.

3. What does Carlos follow into the jungle?
   a. sunflower seeds
   b. a bird
   c. a tour guide
   d. Maya

4. Maya follows a trail of . . .
   a. birds.
   b. stones.
   c. cookies.
   d. sunflower seeds.

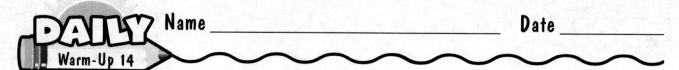

Name _____   Date _____

UNCLE STEVE'S GLASSES

Uncle Steve needed his glasses to read a book. He needed his glasses to drive. But he could not find them.

He looked in his desk drawer. He found a paper clip. He found a rubber band. He even found a stick of gum, but no glasses.

He looked in the bathroom. He found a toothbrush. He found a comb. He even found his missing <u>watch</u>, but no glasses.

Finally, Uncle Steve went to his sister. "Have you seen my glasses?" he asked. "I have looked in the kitchen. I have looked in the bathroom. I cannot find them anywhere!"

His sister laughed and laughed. "Steve," she said, "They are on your head!"

STORY QUESTIONS

1. Uncle Steve needs his glasses to . . .
    a. brush his teeth.
    b. find his sister.
    c. comb his hair.
    d. read a book.

2. What does Uncle Steve find?
    a. a stick
    b. a rubber glove
    c. a watch
    d. a book

3. In this story, *watch* means . . .
    a. stare.
    b. time piece.
    c. look at.
    d. blink.

4. Why does the sister laugh at Uncle Steve?
    a. His glasses are on his head.
    b. His glasses are in his hand.
    c. His glasses are in his desk
    d. He finds his missing watch.

Name _____   Date _____

THE MYSTERIOUS SMELL

Anne rode her bike down the street. She hummed to herself. Then, she stopped. The most delicious smell in the world floated into her nose.

"What is that smell?" she said out loud. She rode to the market on the corner. Mr. Lee sold sweet-smelling tea in little bags. Anne took a big sniff. But that was not the most delicious smell in the world.

Anne rode to Mrs. Miller's house. Mrs. Miller grew roses. Anne <u>stuck</u> her nose into a big red rose. It smelled good, but it was not the most delicious smell in the world.

The smell stayed in her nose all the way home. It followed her to the garage while she put away her bike. It followed as she walked into the kitchen where Dad took a tray of chocolate chip cookies from the oven. Anne smiled. Now she knew what made the most delicious smell in the world!

STORY QUESTIONS

1. For Anne, the most delicious smell comes from . . .
   a. tea.
   b. roses.
   c. cookies.
   d. bikes.

2. What is **true** about this story?
   a. Mr. Lee grows roses.
   b. Mrs. Miller bakes cookies.
   c. Anne takes a sniff of a daisy.
   d. Dad bakes chocolate chip cookies.

3. In this story, *stuck* means . . .
   a. glue.
   b. pushed.
   c. trapped.
   d. paste.

4. The smell of cookies comes from . . .
   a. Anne's kitchen.
   b. the market.
   c. Mrs. Miller's kitchen.
   d. Dad's roses.

DAILY **Name** _____ **Date** _____
Warm-Up 16

RUNWAY GHOST

"Pat to Control Tower. There is a big white object on the runway." Pilot Pat rubbed her eyes. Was it a ghost?

She stopped the plane. Behind her, she could hear people grumbling. Pat felt bad for making them late. But she could not take off with the big white object on the runway. "Control Tower to Pat. We will check it out."

Pat saw three men drive up to the object. They got out of the car. One jumped back. Pat's heart <u>pounded</u>. Suddenly, the big white object rose into the air. It flew off on wide wings. "Ghosts don't have wings," Pat said.

The Control Tower called her. "Control Tower to Pat. The object was a Snowy Owl. It landed on the runway. You're good to go!"

STORY QUESTIONS

1. What lands on the runway?
   a. a ghost   c. an owl
   b. a man   d. a pilot

2. Why does Pat feel bad?
   a. She is sick.   c. She doesn't like ghosts.
   b. She runs over the owl.   d. She will make people late.

3. In this story, *pounded* means . . .
   a. beat.   c. hammer.
   b. smashed.   d. fist.

4. From this story, you know that Snowy Owls are . . .
   a. big and white.
   b. ghosts.
   c. without wings.
   d. airplanes.

THE YOUNG OWL

Once there lived a young owl. All around him, the older owls could hoot. "Whoo, hoo, hoo!" they cried from the trees. But the young owl could not hoot yet. He was not old enough.

He tried and he tried to hoot. He took a deep breath through his beak. He blew out air. But he didn't make a sound. The other owls laughed at him. "I will never be able to hoot," the owl said sadly.

His mother said, "Wait and see, little owl. Very soon, you will have your grown-up voice. Then, you will hoot."

One evening, months later, the young owl awoke in his tree. He opened his eyes to see a crow flying straight toward him. "Who, hoo, hoo are you?" he hooted. The crow flew away. The owl flew after him, hooting happily all the while. His mother had been right!

STORY QUESTIONS

1. Why can't the young owl hoot?
 a. He is too old.
 b. He is a crow.
 c. He is a mother.
 d. He is too young.

2. A beak is an owl's . . .
 a. foot.
 b. mouth.
 c. arm.
 d. wing.

3. What flies straight toward the young owl?
 a. a crow
 b. his mother
 c. another owl
 d. an airplane

4. Why is the young owl happy at the end of the story?
 a. because he can fly
 b. because he can hoot
 c. because he can blow out air
 d. because he is too young

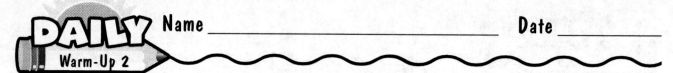

Name _____ Date _____

SAMMY SEAL

Sammy Seal was afraid to swim. He sat on the rocks beside the ocean and watched the other seals swimming. They had a good time doing back flips and racing through the waves. "Come in, Sammy!" they cried. "The water is wonderful!"

Sammy shook his head sadly. "I'm fine here," he said. "I'd rather stay on dry land." Sammy didn't tell anyone the truth. He didn't know how to swim.

But one day, his friend Sue swam up to him. "I'm going to teach you how to swim," she said. "Then, you can have fun with us." Sue showed Sammy how to put one flipper into the water. "Now, put your head in the water," she said.

Sammy put his flippers in the water. Then he put his head in the water. Suddenly, he fell in! For a moment, he was scared. And then he realized something wonderful. "Yeah, Sammy!" cried Sue. "You're swimming!"

STORY QUESTIONS

1. Why is Sammy afraid to swim?
   a. because he is a seal
   b. because he has flippers
   c. because the water is dirty
   d. because he doesn't know how

2. How does Sue help Sammy?
   a. She dumps him in the water.
   b. She teaches him how to swim.
   c. She makes fun of him.
   d. She stays with him on dry land.

3. What happens after Sammy puts his head in the water?
   a. He gets sick.
   b. He falls in.
   c. He cries.
   d. He sits on dry land.

4. The message in this story is . . .
   a. "A good friend is a helpful friend."
   b. "It is scary to swim."
   c. "You should stay on dry land."
   d. "A good friend does not teach you anything."

Name _____ Date _____

THE CLUMSY CAT

Once there was a clumsy cat named Ouch. People say that cats always <u>land</u> on their feet. Not Ouch. She always landed on her head. This is how she got the name "Ouch."

Her brothers and sisters teased her. They jumped down from trees and from roofs. They landed on all four feet. "Jump, Ouch! Jump!" they cried. Ouch jumped down from the tree. She landed on her head. "Ouch!" she said.

With bruises and sores, the clumsy cat went to her father. "I need to learn how to land on my feet," she said.

Father Cat thought and thought. Then he spoke. "Climb up to the top of that tree," he told Ouch. "Jump into the air and do a somersault and a half-twist."

Slowly, Ouch climbed the tree. She jumped into the air. Then she did a somersault and a half-twist. Like magic, she landed on her feet. "Hurrah!" she cried. "Thank you, Father!"

STORY QUESTIONS

1. How does Ouch get her name?
   a. by landing on her head
   b. by landing on her feet
   c. by being angry
   d. by climbing trees

2. In this story, *land* means . . .
   a. ground.
   b. earth.
   c. come to a stop.
   d. get hurt.

3. What word best describes Ouch?
   a. mean
   b. mad
   c. clumsy
   d. dumb

4. Why does Ouch land on her feet?
   a. because she climbs a tree and jumps
   b. because her Father watches
   c. because she does a somersault and a half-twist
   d. because she doesn't like her brothers and sisters

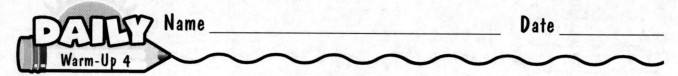

BIG MOUTH

Once there lived a frog named Big Mouth. Big Mouth lived in a pond with many other frogs. He got his name because he loved to gossip about his friends.

Gossip happens when you talk about someone behind his or her back. Big Mouth told everyone that Freddy Frog couldn't hop very high. All the frogs laughed and laughed at Freddy Frog when they saw him. This made Freddy feel sad. But Big Mouth laughed and laughed.

One day Phil Frog got fed up with Big Mouth's big mouth. He said, "Don't gossip, Big Mouth. How would you like it if I told everyone your secret—that you don't like the taste of flies?"

Then, Big Mouth's eyes got big. His big mouth opened into a round "O." "I wouldn't like that at all," he told Phil. Big Mouth never gossiped again.

STORY QUESTIONS

1. Gossip is . . .

   a. a nice thing to do.

   b. a mean thing to do.

   c. only done with frogs.

   d. fun for everyone.

2. Freddy Frog is sad because . . .

   a. Big Mouth makes fun of him.

   b. he doesn't like flies.

   c. he lives in a pond.

   d. he and Phil Frog have a fight.

3. What is Big Mouth's secret?

   a. He can't jump high.

   b. He doesn't like the pond.

   c. He never gossips.

   d. He doesn't like the taste of flies.

4. Why does Big Mouth stop gossiping?

   a. He begins to eat flies.

   b. He moves away from the pond.

   c. He learns that gossip is mean.

   d. Phil told everyone about him.

DAILY Warm-Up 5

Name _____ **Date** _____

CASEY CAN

Mr. and Mrs. Dog had a puppy named Casey. They took him to school. The teacher looked at Casey and said, "Sit."

"I can't," said Casey.

The teacher gave Casey a curious look. "Roll over."

"I can't," said Casey.

Mr. and Mrs. Dog frowned. "Every time we ask Casey to do something, he says he can't," they cried. "Lie down, Casey."

"I can't," said Casey.

The teacher thought and thought. Why couldn't Casey sit or roll over or lie down? Finally, she decided to try something. "Shake hands, please."

At once, Casey held up his brown and black paw for a shake. "I can," he said, "because you said please."

STORY QUESTIONS

1. Why are Mr. and Mrs. Dog upset?
 a. because Casey is dumb
 b. because Casey is mean
 c. because they have a puppy
 d. because Casey won't follow directions

2. What does Casey say when asked to sit?
 a. "I can."
 b. "I can't."
 c. "Roll over."
 d. "Say please."

3. What does Casey's teacher realize?
 a. It's important to say "please."
 b. You have to yell at a student.
 c. No one can roll over.
 d. She doesn't like Casey.

4. Why does Casey shake when asked?
 a. because he is scared of his teacher
 b. because his teacher is polite
 c. because his parents are there
 d. because he is a puppy

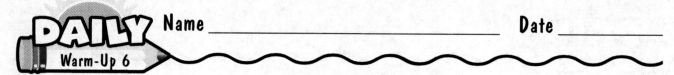

Name _____

Date _____

WANDA WORM

"I'm tired of being a worm," said Wanda one day. "People step on me. They say I am slimy. They say I am gross."

She sat in the mud and cried. She thought about what life would be like if she were pretty like a swan, or strong like a horse.

"Worms are important, too," said Wanda's friend William. He led her out to a trash pile in the backyard. "Watch this!" said William, and he began to eat. He ate melon rinds and apple cores and old moldy lettuce. His body turned the trash into <u>rich</u> black dirt.

"People can use this dirt for planting," William said. "They can plant melons and apple trees and lettuce, thanks to us."

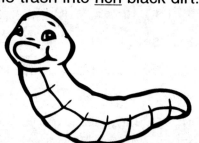

Wanda smiled and began to eat an old carrot. "You're right. Worms are wonderful!" she cried.

STORY QUESTIONS

1. Why are worms wonderful?
   a. because they are gross
   b. because they make rich black dirt
   c. because they are trash
   d. because they are slimy

2. Wanda Worm thinks swans are . . .
   a. trash.   c. pretty.
   b. moldy.   d. strong.

3. What does William show Wanda?
   a. Worms are slimy.   c. Worms are important.
   b. Worms are gross.   d. Worms eat horses.

4. In this story, *rich* means . . .
   a. money.   c. gold.
   b. good.   d. expensive.

DAILY Name _____ Date _____
Warm-Up 7

THE SLOW ELEPHANT

In Africa many animals ran fast. Giraffe ran 30 miles an hour. Lion ran 50 miles an hour. Cheetah ran 70 miles an hour. Elephant could run, but he was slow. "Why can't I be fast?" Elephant cried to Monkey.

"Slow and steady, you see things that fast animals don't," said Monkey. "Wait and see."

One day, the animals met around the water hole. They talked and laughed. Suddenly, they heard a loud "Squeak!" They were scared. They ran as fast as they could.

Elephant tried to catch up. He huffed and puffed, but his legs would not run fast. He had time to look around him. Then, he saw a tiny mouse. "Squeak!" said Mouse. Elephant laughed and laughed.

Monkey nodded from the tree. "You may be slow," he said, "but you see things <u>clearly</u>!"

STORY QUESTIONS

1. Why is Elephant upset?
   a. because he sees a mouse   c. because he sees clearly
   b. because he is fast   d. because he is slow

2. Why do the animals run away?
   a. They hear a noise.   c. They see a monkey.
   b. They see a mouse.   d. They don't like Elephant.

3. Why does Elephant laugh?
   a. because he is so slow
   b. because a little mouse scares the animals
   c. because he sees Monkey
   d. because Mouse squeaks

4. In this story, *clearly* means . . .
   a. plainly.   c. without spots.
   b. with glasses.   d. mice.

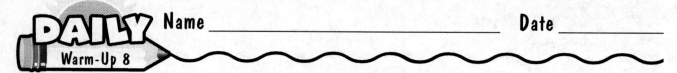

THE SILLY SQUIRREL

In fall all the squirrels in the woods hid acorns. This way, they would have food to eat in the winter. Silly Squirrel hid acorns. But he could not find them again!

Every winter Silly Squirrel had no food to eat. He had to ask his friend Sylvia for some of her acorns. "Silly," said Sylvia, "Why do you lose your acorns?"

Silly thought about this. "I hide them in holes all over the ground. But then I don't know where I put them."

Sylvia gave Silly a leaf. She gave him a rock to use as a pencil. "Make a map of the woods. Then, <u>mark</u> your hiding places with an X."

Silly made a map. Every time he hid an acorn, he marked the hiding place on the map. The next winter he took out his map. Then, he could find his acorns—every single one.

STORY QUESTIONS

1. Why is Silly hungry in the winter?
   a. because he is silly
   b. because he can't find his acorns
   c. because he has a map
   d. because he hides his acorns

2. How does Sylvia help Silly?
   a. She tells him to go away.
   b. She takes acorns from him.
   c. She tells him to make a map.
   d. She hides her acorns.

3. In this story, a *mark* is an . . .
   a. X.
   b. boy.
   c. acorn.
   d. leaf.

4. With a map, Silly can . . .
   a. lose his acorns.
   b. eat Sylvia's acorns.
   c. find his acorns.
   d. get lost.

DAILY
Warm-Up 9

Name _____ Date _____

SATURN'S RINGS

Norm had wanted to go to Saturn since he was a boy. He wanted to see Saturn's rings. "Here, take a look." His father used to point through the telescope. "See Saturn's rings?" But Norm could never see them.

Norm <u>boarded</u> his spaceship. He asked his dog, Star, to come with him. They flew to Saturn.

"I am so happy," said Norm to Star. "Finally, I will see Saturn's rings!"

"Woof!" said Star.

The spaceship landed on Saturn. Norm walked out. All around him, people wore rings in their ears. They wore rings on their fingers. They even wore rings in their noses!

"Well, Star," laughed Norm. "I have seen Saturn's rings!"

"Woof!" said Star.

STORY QUESTIONS

1. Why does Norm want to go to Saturn?
   a. to get an earring   c. to see his father
   b. to drop off Star   d. to see its rings

2. In this story, *boarded* means . . .
   a. wood.   c. hammer and nails.
   b. get inside.   d. tired.

3. On Saturn, people wear rings on their . . .
   a. toes.   c. fingers.
   b. necks.   d. dogs.

4. Star is a . . .
   a. dog.
   b. ring.
   c. spaceship.
   d. person.

Name _____   Date _____

PLANET CAT

John stepped out of the spaceship, and Cat Leader shook his hand. "Nice to meet you," she said. "Welcome to Planet Cat."

John looked around. A cat put down a bowl of milk. A boy licked it with his tongue. Another cat brushed a girl's long ponytail. "What is going on here?" John cried.

Cat Leader purred. "Here, we keep boys and girls as pets."

Then John saw a cat toss a ball of yarn. A girl chased it. He saw another cat put a bell around a boy's arm. "This is so you cannot catch birds," said the cat.

John got back into his spaceship. He headed home to Earth. His cat greeted him at the front door. He gave her a bowl of milk and brushed her fur. "I'm glad you are my pet," he said.

STORY QUESTIONS

1. On Planet Cat, boys and girls are . . .
   a. pets.   c. birds.
   b. cats.   d. aliens.

2. On this planet, cats . . .
   a. chase balls of yarn.   c. catch birds.
   b. lick milk with their tongues.   d. brush people's hair.

3. John lives on Planet . . .
   a. Cat.   c. Bird.
   b. Earth.   d. Space.

4. What is **not true** about this story?
   a. Cats treat girls and boys like pets.
   b. John has a pet cat.
   c. The cats are mean to people.
   d. John lands on Planet Cat.

TROLL FOREST

Have you ever been to Troll Forest? Gus and Lisa found it when they went for a walk. "I've never seen this path," Lisa said. "Let's follow it."

Gus and Lisa walked down a dark path lined with trees. It got darker and darker. They could barely see in front of them. A tiny man jumped out. "Welcome to Troll Forest!" he said. He led them to tiny chairs made out of mushrooms. A little woman gave them cups of hot tea. She gave them cookies that were smaller than Gus' thumbnail.

Gus and Lisa watched Baby Troll crawl around on moss. It was too dark to leave Troll Forest that night, so they slept on a soft bed of leaves. In the morning, the trolls made them mushroom pancakes, then showed them the path back to their home. "Come back to Troll Forest," they called after Gus and Lisa. "See you soon!"

STORY QUESTIONS

1. Troll Forest is in . . .
- a. the ocean.
- b. the middle of Earth.
- c. the forest.
- d. the desert.

2. The people in Troll Forest are . . .
- a. very tall.
- b. tiny.
- c. not kind.
- d. heavy.

3. Where do Lisa and Gus sleep?
- a. in a feather bed
- b. on leaves
- c. on moss
- d. on a mushroom

4. From this story, you can tell that . . .
- a. the trolls don't like Gus and Lisa.
- b. the trolls do not share their food.
- c. the trolls want Gus and Lisa to visit again.
- d. Gus and Lisa are afraid of the trolls.

DAILY Name _____ Date _____
Warm-Up 12

EMILY'S ROCKET

Emily wanted to build a rocket. "I will go to Mars," she said. "I will go to Pluto. I will even visit the moon."

Scotty laughed. "You don't know how to build a rocket!"

"I'll show you," said Emily. She found some wood and some nails. She found a hammer. She found an old pie tin and some bike pedals. She began to work.

At last, Emily was done. "Turn these bike pedals," she told Scotty. She climbed into the rocket.

He laughed again. "This will never work," he said. But he turned the pedals.

Suddenly, Emily was gone! The rocket shot straight up into the air. It landed on Mars, and Emily stepped out. "I showed you!" she called down to Scotty on Earth.

But he was gone. He'd made a rocket of his own, and he was waiting for Emily on Pluto.

STORY QUESTIONS

1. Why does Scotty laugh at Emily?
   a. He thinks she can build a rocket.
   b. He thinks her plan is silly.
   c. He wants to eat pie.
   d. He wants to ride his bike.

2. Emily makes her rocket out of . . .
   a. flowers.
   b. bikes.
   c. wood, tin, and bike pedals.
   d. wood, pie, and bike tires.

3. What happens when Scotty turns the pedals?
   a. The rocket crashes.
   b. Nothing.
   c. The rocket goes to Pluto.
   d. The rocket shoots into the air.

4. What is **true** about this story?
   a. Emily laughs at Scotty.
   b. Emily can not use a hammer.
   c. Emily is creative.
   d. Scott stops Emily from going.

DAILY Warm-Up 13 **Name** _____ **Date** _____

GLENDA GOLDFISH

Glenda was a goldfish. She lived in a bowl on Nick's desk. She had fresh water. She had a little castle. But she was bored. "I want to swim in the ocean," Glenda said. "I want to see the world."

One night it got windy. Nick forgot to close his window. The wind was so strong that it picked Glenda up out of her bowl. The rain <u>washed</u> her into the gutter. She floated along until she came to the ocean!

"At last!" said Glenda. "I can see the world!"

But she was a small fish, and the world was very big. A whale tried to eat her. She missed her castle. "I wish I could go back to my bowl," Glenda said. She swam out of the ocean and back up the gutter. She waited in a puddle outside Nick's house. When he saw her, he smiled. "You came back!" he cried and put her back in her bowl.

STORY QUESTIONS

1. Where does Glenda live?
    a. in the gutter   c. in a desk
    b. in a puddle   d. in a bowl

2. Why does Glenda want to see the world?
    a. She is bored.   c. She is a whale.
    b. She does not like Nick.   d. She does not have fresh water.

3. In this story, *washed* means
    a. soap and water.   c. laundry.
    b. pushed.   d. castle.

4. Where does Nick find Glenda?
    a. in a castle
    b. in a gutter
    c. in a puddle
    d. in the ocean

DAILY
Warm-Up 14

Name _____

Date _____

GOING TO EARTH

Minnie wanted to see Earth. She was tired of Mars. "Same old red dirt," she said. "Same old dusty land." But Minnie's father wouldn't let her drive the spaceship.

"You are not old enough," Dad said.

Minnie knew how to drive. Her older brother had taught her. One day she got into the spaceship and turned the key. "To Earth!" she said.

The spaceship took Minnie all the way to Earth. She got out and walked on green grass. "Earth is pretty!" she cried. "Oops!" Minnie was so busy looking at a river that she slipped in mud. The key to the spaceship fell into the river. It was lost. "How will I go home?" she cried.

Just then, she heard a voice. She turned to find Dad standing there. He had a key in his hand. "Good thing we have an extra spaceship," he said.

STORY QUESTIONS

1. Why does Minnie want to see Earth?
a. She wants to move there.
b. She doesn't like her father.
c. She doesn't know how to drive.
d. She is tired of Mars.

2. Who teaches Minnie how to drive?
a. her father
b. her mother
c. her older brother
d. her younger brother

3. The key falls into the . . .
a. river.
b. mud.
c. spaceship.
d. dirt.

4. Minnie's father brings her another . . .
a. Earth.
b. key.
c. spanking.
d. brother.

DAILY Warm-Up 15   **Name** _____   **Date** _____

ANT BOY

There was a boy who liked to step on ants. He went out of his way to step on them. "Ants do not matter," he said.

One morning, the boy woke up to find that he had six legs. He had strong jaws, but he could not eat solid food. He could only drink juice. "I am an ant!" the boy cried.

The boy was very small. He could not get dressed because his pants only had room for two legs. He tried to crawl to school, but he had only reached his front door when the bell for nine o'clock rang.

"I'm late!" cried the boy. He tried to run as fast as his six legs would carry him. Then, a dark shadow loomed over him. He looked up and saw the sole of a shoe.

"Oh no!" cried the boy. "Please do not step on me! Ants do matter!"

The next day, he woke up, and he was back to being a boy. But he never stepped on ants again.

STORY QUESTIONS

1. The boy in the story likes to . . .
   a. drink juice.
   b. step on pants.
   c. save ants.
   d. step on ants.

2. From this story, you learn that ants . . .
   a. can step on people.
   b. cannot eat solid food.
   c. have eight legs.
   d. do not matter.

3. Why can't the boy put on his pants?
   a. Someone steps on them.
   b. He has six legs.
   c. He has a strong jaw.
   d. He cannot find them.

4. Why does the boy stop stepping on ants?
   a. He finds that they do matter.
   b. He wakes up.
   c. He cannot find his shoes.
   d. He is late.

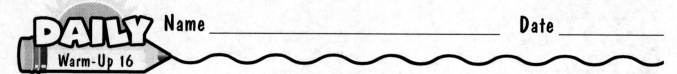

RITA'S FLIGHT

Rita loved birds. When she found a hurt crow, she cared for it until it was well. She hung bird feeders from her trees. She put birdbaths full of water in her backyard.

But Rita was sad. "I wish I could fly," she said to herself. A Robin nearby heard Rita's wish. He went to the other birds.

"Rita is good to us," Robin said. "Can we help her fly?"

"But we're so small," said Crow. "What can we do?"

The birds came up with a plan. One day, Rita stood outside tossing seed for the birds. Suddenly, two Golden Eagles swooped down. They caught Rita gently under her arms and flew up to the sky with her. For hours, they flew her all over the town and the hills. Rita never forgot that flight, and she never forgot to put food out for the birds.

STORY QUESTIONS

1. What does Rita do for the birds?
   a. She eats them.
   b. She feeds them.
   c. She gives them juice.
   d. She clips their wings.

2. What does Rita wish for?
   a. seeds
   b. water
   c. eagles
   d. flight

3. Who flies with Rita?
   a. Crow
   b. Golden Eagles
   c. Robin
   d. Bald Eagles

4. From this story, you can tell that . . .
   a. Rita is not afraid of heights.
   b. Rita does not like birds.
   c. the birds are scared of Rita.
   d. Rita does not like to fly.

ANSWER KEY

168   ©Teacher Created Resources, Inc.

Answer Key

Nonfiction

Animals

Page 9 Great-horned Owls
1. b
2. a
3. d
4. d

Page 10 Cats
1. c
2. b
3. d
4. a

Page 11 The Crow
1. b
2. c
3. a
4. d

Page 12 The Polar Bear
1. c
2. b
3. a
4. d

Page 13 Dogs
1. b
2. d
3. c
4. d

Page 14 Emperor Penguin
1. c
2. b
3. d
4. a

Page 15 Gila Monster
1. b
2. d
3. a
4. c

Page 16 Millipedes
1. b
2. c
3. a
4. c

Page 17 Ivory-billed Woodpecker
1. d
2. c
3. a
4. c

Page 18 Peregrine Falcon
1. b
2. c
3. a
4. d

Page 19 Anteater
1. a
2. b
3. d
4. a

Page 20 Stinkbug
1. c
2. d
3. b
4. a

Page 21 Giant Panda
1. c
2. b
3. a
4. d

Page 22 Black Widow
1. b
2. d
3. a
4. a

Page 23 Giraffe
1. d
2. b
3. d
4. a

Geography

Page 24 The Ocean
1. b
2. c
3. a
4. d

Page 25 Mountains
1. c
2. d
3. b
4. a

Page 26 Trees
1. c
2. a
3. b
4. d

Page 27 Rivers
1. a
2. c
3. d
4. b

Page 28 Deserts
1. b
2. d
3. a
4. d

Page 29 Wetlands
1. c
2. b
3. d
4. a

Page 30 Glaciers
1. d
2. a
3. b
4. b

Page 31 Rainforests
1. d
2. b
3. c
4. a

Page 32 Volcanoes
1. c
2. d
3. a
4. d

Page 33 Canyons
1. c
2. a
3. d
4. b

Page 34 Earthquakes
1. b
2. d
3. a
4. c

Page 35 Tornadoes
1. c
2. a
3. d
4. b

Answer Key

Page 36 Hurricanes
1. d
2. b
3. c
4. a

Page 37 Tsunami
1. c
2. c
3. a
4. d

Page 38 Blizzards
1. c
2. a
3. a
4. c

Science

Page 39 Sun, Earth, and Moon
1. b
2. c
3. d
4. c

Page 40 Fossils
1. c
2. a
3. b
4. a

Page 41 Worms
1. c
2. b
3. c
4. a

Page 42 Trees
1. d
2. b
3. c
4. a

Page 43 Lightning
1. d
2. b
3. d
4. c

Page 44 Butterfly
1. c
2. b
3. a
4. c

Page 45 Fall Leaves
1. c
2. b
3. a
4. d

Page 46 Where Animals Go
1. a
2. d
3. c
4. b

Page 47 Stars
1. c
2. c
3. b
4. a

Page 48 The Moon
1. b
2. a
3. c
4. d

Page 49 Sharks
1. c
2. b
3. d
4. c

Page 50 The Food Chain
1. c
2. a
3. c
4. a

Page 51 Venus Fly Trap
1. b
2. d
3. a
4. c

Page 52 Dust
1. c
2. b
3. d
4. a

Page 53 Rainbows
1. c
2. a
3. c
4. d

Page 54 Inventions
1. d
2. b
3. a
4. b

American History

Page 55 American Colonies
1. c
2. b
3. d
4. d

Page 56 Betsy Ross
1. d
2. c
3. b
4. a

Page 57 The Bald Eagle
1. b
2. d
3. a
4. b

Page 58 Bison
1. d
2. b
3. a
4. b

Page 59 Uncle Sam
1. d
2. c
3. b
4. d

Page 60 Yankee Doodle
1. c
2. b
3. a
4. c

Page 61 Johnny Appleseed
1. c
2. a
3. d
4. c

Page 62 Fireworks
1. d
2. b
3. a
4. c

Answer Key

Page 63   George Washington
1. b
2. c
3. d
4. a

Page 64   Abe Lincoln
1. a
2. c
3. b
4. c

Page 65   Sacagawea
1. c
2. b
3. a
4. d

Page 66   Harriet Tubman
1. d
2. b
3. b
4. d

Page 67   The Mayans
1. b
2. b
3. a
4. b

Page 68   Space Travel
1. b
2. c
3. a
4. b

Health and Wellness

Page 69   Germs
1. c
2. b
3. d
4. a

Page 70   Exercise
1. c
2. b
3. a
4. d

Page 71   Healthy Food
1. b
2. c
3. d
4. a

Page 72   Ears
1. d
2. a
3. b
4. a

Page 73   Lungs
1. c
2. a
3. c
4. c

Page 74   Sleep
1. d
2. a
3. b
4. c

Page 75   Water
1. b
2. a
3. d
4. c

Page 76   Teeth
1. c
2. b
3. a
4. d

Page 77   Bones
1. c
2. a
3. c
4. b

Page 78   Common Cold
1. b
2. c
3. d
4. c

Page 79   Chicken Pox
1. d
2. a
3. b
4. c

Page 80   Eyes
1. b
2. d
3. d
4. a

Page 81   Getting Mad
1. a
2. b
3. d
4. d

Page 82   Bruises
1. b
2. c
3. a
4. d

Page 83   Laughter
1. d
2. b
3. c
4. c

Page 84   Allergies
1. c
2. b
3. a
4. d

Page 85   Foods with Color
1. c
2. a
3. d
4. a

Page 86   Talk It Out
1. b
2. c
3. a
4. d

Fiction
Fairy Tales and Folklore

Page 89   The Farmer's Corn
1. b
2. c
3. a
4. d

Page 90   The Fisherwoman
1. c
2. b
3. d
4. c

Page 91   Talking Trees
1. c
2. b
3. a
4. d

Page 92 The Sharing Man
1. b
2. c
3. a
4. b

Page 93 The Royal Wedding
1. c
2. d
3. a
4. a

Page 94 The Strong Princess
1. d
2. b
3. a
4. c

Page 95 King Cheese
1. b
2. c
3. a
4. a

Page 96 Paul Bunyan's Dinner
1. d
2. c
3. a
4. a

Page 97 Prince Peter's Peas
1. d
2. a
3. c
4. c

Page 98 Vulcan's Fire
1. b
2. d
3. b
4. c

Page 99 Davy's Hat
1. d
2. b
3. b
4. a

Page 100 Athena's Owl
1. c
2. a
3. c
4. a

Page 101 Bigfoot!
1. d
2. b
3. c
4. a

Page 102 Annie's Cat
1. c
2. a
3. b
4. d

Page 103 Looking for a Head
1. d
2. b
3. a
4. b

Historical Fiction
Page 104 The Ugly Boy
1. b
2. c
3. a
4. d

Page 105 Quentin's Pony
1. d
2. b
3. c
4. d

Page 106 The Lady with a Lamp
1. c
2. b
3. d
4. a

Page 107 The Red Flower
1. d
2. b
3. b
4. a

Page 108 I Dare You
1. a
2. c
3. c
4. b

Page 109 The Good Mother
1. c
2. b
3. d
4. a

Page 110 The Bathtub
1. b
2. a
3. b
4. b

Page 111 Rosa on the Bus
1. d
2. c
3. b
4. a

Page 112 Franklin's Problem
1. b
2. b
3. a
4. d

Page 113 Anne's Diary
1. a
2. b
3. c
4. b

Page 114 The Girl Painter
1. d
2. d
3. c
4. b

Page 115 Mozart and Music
1. c
2. a
3. b
4. d

Page 116 Smokey the Bear
1. c
2. a
3. d
4. d

Page 117 Pat's Music
1. d
2. b
3. a
4. b

Page 118 Kat's Poem
1. c
2. a
3. a
4. d

Answer Key

Page 119 The Liberty Bell
1. d
2. d
3. d
4. a

Contemporary Realistic Fiction

Page 120 Stuart's Stuff
1. b
2. d
3. a
4. d

Page 121 The Small Girl
1. d
2. a
3. b
4. a

Page 122 Mark
1. a
2. c
3. a
4. c

Page 123 Tamales
1. c
2. d
3. a
4. b

Page 124 The Dog
1. b
2. c
3. c
4. a

Page 125 The Firefighter
1. d
2. b
3. c
4. a

Page 126 Grandma Is Sick
1. b
2. d
3. a
4. a

Page 127 The Bean Plant
1. b
2. d
3. a
4. b

Page 128 The Stray Cat
1. b
2. d
3. a
4. c

Page 129 New Baby
1. c
2. d
3. b
4. a

Page 130 The Airplane
1. a
2. a
3. a
4. d

Page 131 The Computer
1. a
2. c
3. d
4. b

Page 132 Spiders
1. c
2. a
3. d
4. a

Page 133 The Lie
1. a
2. b
3. d
4. c

Page 134 Frank's Bedroom
1. c
2. a
3. d
4. c

Mystery/Suspense/Adventure

Page 135 Going Camping
1. b
2. d
3. d
4. b

Page 136 The Nest
1. d
2. c
3. b
4. d

Page 137 The Kitten
1. d
2. b
3. b
4. a

Page 138 Surfer Jin
1. c
2. b
3. a
4. c

Page 139 The Adventure
1. c
2. d
3. a
4. b

Page 140 The Note
1. d
2. b
3. a
4. c

Page 141 The Apple Thief
1. d
2. d
3. b
4. a

Page 142 Scary Story
1. d
2. a
3. c
4. b

Page 143 School Mice
1. c
2. d
3. b
4. a

Page 144 Lost Dog
1. c
2. c
3. a
4. c

Page 145 Dots of Flour
1. d
2. b
3. a
4. c

Answer Key

Page 146 The Green Eyes
1. b
2. d
3. a
4. b

Page 147 The Jungle
1. a
2. c
3. b
4. d

Page 148 Uncle Steve's Glasses
1. d
2. c
3. b
4. a

Page 149 The Mysterious Smell
1. c
2. d
3. b
4. a

Page 150 Runway Ghost
1. c
2. d
3. a
4. a

Fantasy

Page 151 The Young Owl
1. d
2. b
3. a
4. b

Page 152 Sammy Seal
1. d
2. b
3. b
4. a

Page 153 The Clumsy Cat
1. a
2. c
3. c
4. c

Page 154 Big Mouth
1. b
2. a
3. d
4. c

Page 155 Casey Can
1. d
2. b
3. a
4. b

Page 156 Wanda Worm
1. b
2. c
3. c
4. b

Page 157 The Slow Elephant
1. d
2. a
3. b
4. a

Page 158 The Silly Squirrel
1. b
2. c
3. a
4. c

Page 159 Saturn's Rings
1. d
2. b
3. c
4. a

Page 160 Planet Cat
1. a
2. d
3. b
4. c

Page 161 Troll Forest
1. c
2. b
3. b
4. c

Page 162 Emily's Rocket
1. b
2. c
3. d
4. c

Page 163 Glenda Goldfish
1. d
2. a
3. b
4. c

Page 164 Going to Earth
1. d
2. c
3. a
4. b

Page 165 Ant Boy
1. d
2. b
3. b
4. a

Page 166 Rita's Flight
1. b
2. d
3. b
4. a

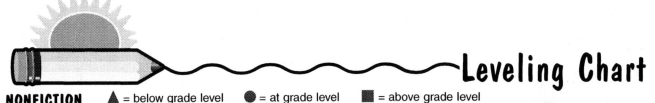

Leveling Chart

NONFICTION ▲ = below grade level ● = at grade level ■ = above grade level

Animals		Geography		Science		American History		Health and Wellness	
Page 9	●	Page 24	■	Page 39	■	Page 55	●	Page 69	●
Page 10	●	Page 25	●	Page 40	●	Page 56	●	Page 70	●
Page 11	▲	Page 26	▲	Page 41	●	Page 57	■	Page 71	■
Page 12	■	Page 27	●	Page 42	■	Page 58	●	Page 72	●
Page 13	●	Page 28	●	Page 43	■	Page 59	●	Page 73	■
Page 14	■	Page 29	●	Page 44	●	Page 60	●	Page 74	●
Page 15	●	Page 30	●	Page 45	●	Page 61	●	Page 75	●
Page 16	●	Page 31	●	Page 46	●	Page 62	●	Page 76	●
Page 17	■	Page 32	●	Page 47	●	Page 63	■	Page 77	■
Page 18	■	Page 33	●	Page 48	■	Page 64	●	Page 78	●
Page 19	●	Page 34	▲	Page 49	●	Page 65	■	Page 79	●
Page 20	●	Page 35	■	Page 50	●	Page 66	●	Page 80	■
Page 21	●	Page 36	●	Page 51	■	Page 67	■	Page 81	●
Page 22	●	Page 37	●	Page 52	●	Page 68	●	Page 82	▲
Page 23	●	Page 38	●	Page 53	■			Page 83	●
				Page 54	●			Page 84	■
								Page 85	■
								Page 86	●

FICTION ▲ = below grade level ● = at grade level ■ = above grade level

Fairy Tales and Folklore		Historical Fiction		Contemporary Realistic Fiction		Mystery/Suspense/Adventure		Fantasy	
Page 89	●	Page 104	●	Page 120	●	Page 135	▲	Page 151	●
Page 90	●	Page 105	■	Page 121	●	Page 136	●	Page 152	●
Page 91	■	Page 106	●	Page 122	▲	Page 137	●	Page 153	▲
Page 92	●	Page 107	●	Page 123	■	Page 138	●	Page 154	■
Page 93	●	Page 108	●	Page 124	●	Page 139	●	Page 155	●
Page 94	●	Page 109	●	Page 125	●	Page 140	▲	Page 156	■
Page 95	▲	Page 110	●	Page 126	▲	Page 141	●	Page 157	●
Page 96	●	Page 111	●	Page 127	▲	Page 142	▲	Page 158	■
Page 97	●	Page 112	●	Page 128	●	Page 143	●	Page 159	●
Page 98	●	Page 113	●	Page 129	●	Page 144	▲	Page 160	▲
Page 99	▲	Page 114	●	Page 130	●	Page 145	●	Page 161	■
Page 100	▲	Page 115	●	Page 131	■	Page 146	▲	Page 162	●
Page 101	●	Page 116	▲	Page 132	●	Page 147	●	Page 163	●
Page 102	●	Page 117	●	Page 133	▲	Page 148	●	Page 164	●
Page 103	●	Page 118	■	Page 134	▲	Page 149	●	Page 165	▲
		Page 119	●			Page 150	●	Page 166	●

Congratulations
to

_____

for completing

_____

_____

_____
Signature

_____
Date